Sentence Construction

WRITING, COMBINING, AND EDITING STANDARD ENGLISH SENTENCES

Book I

SECOND EDITION

Lynn E. Henrichsen • *Alice C. Pack*

BRIGHAM YOUNG UNIVERSITY, HAWAII CAMPUS

Heinle & Heinle Publishers
A Division of Wadsworth, Inc.
Boston, Massachusetts 02116

Publisher: Stanley J. Galek
Editorial Director: David C. Lee
Project Editor: Ros Herion Freese
Editorial Production Manager: Elizabeth Holthaus
Production Editor: Kristin Thalheimer
Manufacturing Coordinator: Lisa McLaughlin
Interior Design: Ros Herion Freese
Cover Design: Robert Pehlke

Sentence Construction: Writing, Combining, and Editing Standard English Sentences

Heinle & Heinle Publishers is a division of Wadsworth, Inc.

Manufactured in the United States of America.

Library of Congress Cataloging-in-Publication Data

Henrichsen, Lynn E.
    Writing, combining, and editing standard English sentences / Lynn E. Henrichsen, Alice C. Pack. -- 2nd ed.
        p.   cm.
    Rev. ed. of: Writing and combining standard English sentences / Alice C. Pack, Lynn E. Henrichsen. 1980–
    Contents: bk. 1. Sentence construction -- bk. 2. Sentence combination.
    ISBN 0-8384-3015-5. -- ISBN 0-8384-3017-1
    1. English language--Textbooks for foreign speakers. 2. English language--Sentences. 3. English language--Rhetoric. I. Pack, Alice C. II. Pack, Alice C. Writing and combining standard English sentences. III. Title.
PE1128.H432 1992   91-44906
    428.2'4--dc20   CIP

ISBN 0-8384-3015-5

10 9 8 7 6 5 4 3 2 1

Contents

5. Verb Forms and Their Uses   83

6. Verbs and Time   109

7. The Sentence   147

Chapters in Book II, *Sentence Combination:*

Why This Book Uses "New" Grammar Terms

In *Sentence Construction* (and *Sentence Combination*) you will occasionally encounter terms like *aux-word, shifter, dummy subject,* and *d-t-n form,* which may be unfamiliar to you. There are two important reasons why these terms are used.

✸ **Of the many varying grammar terms, those used in this book have proven most helpful to students.**

Even among traditional grammar experts, there is considerable variation regarding terminology. For example, what *Sentence Construction* calls a "dummy subject" is called many different things in other grammar books—"anticipatory *it* as subject," "impersonal *it,*" or "*it* expletive." What *Sentence Combination* calls a "half-sentence" various other books call a "participial phrase," "nonfinite verb clause in which the verb is an *-ing* participle," "*-ing* clause without a subject," "absolute construction," "nominative absolute," or "disjunctive dependent clause." In preparing *Sentence Construction* and *Sentence Combination,* a choice had to be made regarding the use of these terms.*

The principle guiding this choice was to use the clearest, most descriptive terms possible. Sometimes this meant using traditional terms. In other cases, however, traditional terms were not satisfactory. For instance, the term *present participle* is not used in the books because it is misleading. (The *-ing form* is actually timeless and can be used in both present and past tenses.) In other cases, however, traditional grammar terms have been employed, or new, compromise terms have been coined.

• **The new terms are part of the process of helping you gain a new understanding of how modern, written English actually works.**

The use of these new terms involves more than just putting new labels on the same old grammar points. As you study the explanations in *Sentence Construction* and *Sentence Combination,* you will realize that there are additional differences in the ways they explain the system of English.

For instance, many of the explanations employ a grammar system called "sector analysis," which was specially designed for teaching the mechanics of modern, written English. Others use a tense-aspect approach to explain English verbs and time relationships. These nontraditional approaches have been adopted because they have proven more effective than traditional Latin-based or nonpedagogically oriented approaches to teaching students how written English works. One of the books' great strengths is that, besides being more easily taught and learned, the new perspective on English grammar that they present reflects the actual workings of modern, written English more accurately.

For example, in Latin-based grammar the traditional approach to parts of speech barely recognizes the auxiliary (calling it a "helping verb") and relegates it to a secondary, supporting role. Nevertheless, as English has evolved in recent centuries, the auxiliary has taken on a variety of powerful and pervasive functions,

---

*Many explanations do mention alternate terms, and Appendix F lists additional "translations" of grammar terms.

becoming all but indispensable for question and negative formation, serving to mark emphasis in written English, and frequently functioning as a substitute for the entire predicate. These are roles that the auxiliary did not play in modern English's ancestral forms, nor in most other languages, and certainly not in Latin, the language on which traditional grammar is based. Sector analysis, however, gives the "aux-word" the emphasis that its importance in modern English merits.

Likewise, the infinitive form and the subjunctive mood of verbs, which are so important in Latin and many Romance languages, simply do not have parallel functions in modern English. While not ignoring these grammar points (the different uses of infinitives are treated in Chapters 5, 7, and 13, and the subjunctive is mentioned in Chapter 13), the grammar explanations in *Sentence Construction* and *Sentence Combination* recognize these differences and treat these grammar points accordingly.

If you are accustomed to some version of traditional, Latin-based grammar, you may find the nontraditional grammar explanations and terminology used in *Sentence Construction* and *Sentence Combination* somewhat different at first. Nevertheless, experience using these books with thousands of students for over ten years has demonstrated that if you accept these new approaches and learn to understand and use them, they will help you.

To the Student

This book focuses on selected "trouble spots"—areas in which most non-native users of standard English experience persistent difficulty when they write. Although it reviews many basics in English grammar, this book is not intended for beginners in English.

If you are like most intermediate to advanced students, you still have occasional trouble with English verb forms and tenses, articles, nouns and pronouns, word forms, and/or sentence structure. This book is designed to help you overcome these difficulties and produce correct basic sentences. In addition, the understanding of English grammar that you gain from this book will help you to eliminate errors and improve what you have written as you proofread and edit your sentences.

After you have learned to write correct simple sentences, *Sentence Combination* (Book II in this series) will teach you a variety of methods for combining them into complex, mature sentences.

As noted in the preceding section, both books employ a grammar called "sector analysis," a system specially designed for teaching the mechanics of modern, written English. They also use a tense-aspect approach to explain English verbs and time relationships. Thousands of students from various linguistic, cultural, and educational backgrounds have used these approaches with great success. They now write English with fewer errors and greater confidence. You can too.

To the Teacher

This book focuses on selected aspects of written English that are especially difficult for most intermediate and advanced students of English as a second language (and standard English as a second dialect). These areas of persistent difficulty include derivational and inflectional endings of content words, articles and their use with various types of nouns, pronoun usage, basic sentence structure, the complex auxiliary and verb system of modern English, and the different time relationships this system indicates.

The primary purpose of this volume and its companion, *Sentence Combination*, is to teach students to write grammatically correct, expository prose of the type generally expected in academic situations. Besides helping them produce correct written English, the conscious knowledge of grammar rules that students gain from the explanations and exercises in these books will also help them as they proofread, "monitor," and edit their writing.

In *Sentence Construction*, student production is limited to writing and editing correct basic sentences. *Sentence Combination* teaches numerous sentence-building, transforming, and combining techniques that students can employ to produce complexity, variety, and maturity in their writing.

Explanatory sections are kept as brief, nontechnical, and student-oriented as possible. They are broken down into small, sequenced increments and accompanied by numerous examples as well as explanatory charts and diagrams.

As noted above, many of the explanations are nontraditional. Some are based on sector analysis, a special pedagogical grammar of written English designed by Professor Robert L. Allen of Teachers College, Columbia University. Those dealing with verbs and time rely heavily on the tense-aspect system elaborated by Professor William E. Bull of the University of California at Los Angeles. These new approaches have been adopted because they have proven more effective than traditional Latin-based or nonpedagogically oriented approaches to teaching students how written English works.

When it has proven useful by virtue of being more descriptive or clear, new terminology has also been adopted. In other cases, however, traditional grammar terms have been employed, or new, compromise terms have been coined. The guiding principle in all these decisions has been to use what is most helpful in making English grammar clear to students.

The primary pedagogical principle behind the design of these books is that students learn by doing. In other words, they learn to write by writing, and they gain more from practice writing exercises than they do from a teacher's explanatory presentations. Nevertheless, clear guidance from a teacher can make students' practice more effective. Therefore, in *Sentence Construction* and *Sentence Combination*, brief, focused explanations are followed by generously long sets of assignments. Grammar explanations are limited to what is pedagogically useful with the expectation that most learning will take place as students work through assignments. Teachers are urged to bear this principle in mind and keep their explanatory presentations brief, simple, and to the point, even if they tend to be somewhat general. Students can always go back and read the explanations in the book if they need detailed guidance. In fact, they will probably learn better and remember longer the things they learn when looking for the answer to a question. For this reason, during and after the time when students are working on the practice exercises in class, the teacher should allow time for the discussion of details and the answering of questions from students.

Additional guidelines and suggestions for using *Sentence Construction* and *Sentence Combination* are provided in the teacher's manual (available from the publisher). This guide also provides diagnostic material, an answer key for the exercises, and an achievement test for each chapter in *Sentence Construction*.

Preface to the Second Edition

Those familiar with the first edition of *Sentence Construction* and *Sentence Combination* will notice a number of improvements in this second edition. These revisions reflect over ten years of experience in using the first edition with students from a wide variety of linguistic, cultural, and educational backgrounds. Overall, the modifications have the effect of eliminating the first edition's weaknesses while maintaining its strengths and building new ones. The books are now not only easier to use but more effective in helping students master the challenges of writing, combining, and editing English sentences.

A number of changes reflect recognition of the fact that writing is a process that involves writing and rewriting. Changes in this new edition encourage students to follow the same "monitoring," proofreading, and editing processes that good writers typically go through. In this regard, the need for a conscious understanding of grammar rules, which *Sentence Construction* and *Sentence Combination* have always developed, gains a new rationale as a tool for evaluating what one has already written. Additional, new features, such as the display of sample mistakes (actual student errors in most cases) at the beginning of each chapter and the proofreading exercises at the end of the first six chapters, emphasize and encourage these rewriting processes.

Another major improvement is the provision of a teacher's manual, which provides guidance for using *Sentence Construction* and *Sentence Combination*, a more detailed rationale for the approach they employ, an answer key for the exercises, and achievement tests for each chapter in *Sentence Construction*.

Although explanations in both books continue to rely on sector analysis and the tense-aspect system of English auxiliaries and verbs, many of them have been rewritten to improve their clarity and their completeness. In addition, a few new sections have been added, such as the one that explains the use of verb tenses to show real and unreal conditions.

The exercises as a whole maintain the continuous-context feature that makes them more natural and realistic. Nevertheless, many old exercises have been modified and a number of new ones created. Some of these new exercises support the explanations in the newly added sections, but most either replace old exercises that were outdated or less effective or provide additional practice in areas in which students experience greater difficulty and thus need extra practice. In several cases, student response procedures have also been modified to make the exercises easier to use and/or correct.

Another major difference between the first and second editions is the location of the chapter on modifiers, which is now in Book II, *Sentence Combination*. This change recognizes the fact that many of the procedures taught in this chapter involve sentence combining. It also allows Book I, *Sentence Construction*, to end at a more natural point (the sentence). Furthermore, it evens out the length of the two books, making them more suitable for many semester/quarter calendars.

The single, most important reason behind all these changes was to make the books more effective in the classroom. Suggestions from users of *Sentence Construction* and *Sentence Combination* regarding additional improvements are always welcome and should be sent to Dr. Lynn E. Henrichsen [Language, Literature and Communications Division, Brigham Young University–Hawaii, Laie, HI 96762-1294 (USA)].

L.E.H.

Acknowledgments

We are deeply indebted to the numerous friends, colleagues, and students who have worked with us during the production and revision of *Sentence Construction* and *Sentence Combination*. Without their helpful advice and enthusiastic encouragement, the dream which these books represent would never have become a reality.

First of all, we want to thank the many students in the English Language Institute at Brigham Young University–Hawaii and at the Universidad Autónoma de Chihuahua who used trial versions of the materials. They represent over 50 different mother tongues, and their reactions and suggestions have proven extremely useful.

Over the years, many teachers have used *Sentence Construction* and *Sentence Combination* and offered constructive ideas for using and improving them. These helpful colleagues are simply too numerous to name, but we thank them all.

Fortunate is the teacher who works at a school where the administration encourages creativity in teaching and promotes the development of new materials that better fit students' educational needs. For support of this nature, we are grateful to the administration of Brigham Young University–Hawaii. In particular, we thank the directors of its English Language Institute, Earl Wyman and Norman Evans, who allowed the trial use of preliminary revisions of *Sentence Construction* and *Sentence Combination* in ELI courses for several semesters.

Special appreciation is due to various members of the Newbury House and the Heinle & Heinle editorial staffs who helped us through the long process of producing this second edition: Laurie Likoff, who got us started; Kathleen Ossip, who kept us going; and David Lee and Anne Sokolsky, who saw things through to completion.

The comments of the reviewers of the semifinal revised manuscript were also very helpful and much appreciated. Therefore, we wish to thank: Ulysses D'Aguila (Alemany Community College), Christine Bauer-Ramazani (St. Michael's College), Ellen Lewin (Minneapolis Community College), Ann Ludwig (University of Nebraska), Monica Maxwell (Georgetown University), and Mark Picus (Houston Community College).

Finally, we extend our deepest thanks to our families for their endless patience and cheerful sacrifices. This section would be deplorably incomplete if it failed to acknowledge the unflagging support and willing assistance of Terumi, Cristina, Daniel, Linda, and James during the years it took to complete the revision.

L.E.H.
A.C.P.

1

Word Types
and Forms

This chapter will help you avoid or correct mistakes like these:

- My mother looks very young and <u>beauty</u>.
- I really like <u>China</u> food.
- Burma is a <u>Buddhism</u> country.
- Electricity was mastered in the <u>nineteen</u> century.
- Without electricity, the world would become a <u>darkness</u> place.
- I have a friend who is a famous <u>architecture</u>.
- I am very <u>thanks</u> for your letter.
- He talked about the pursuit of <u>true</u> in all things.

1. Content and Function Words

In English there are two types of words: (1) content words, and (2) function words.

Content Words	Function Words
book	a
diesel	the
archaeology	of
read	and
elephant	or
typewriter	not
quickly	when
horrible	about
man	under

The number of function words is very small (about 150) when compared with the large number of content words (hundreds of thousands and continually increasing). Nevertheless, function words are used very frequently and must be used precisely in written English. You are not expected to know all the content words in English (nobody does), but you must understand and use nearly all the function words.

The following sentences show how content and function words are used.

> The man quickly read a book about archaeology.
> F   C   C   C   F C   F   C
>
> Clark studied the history of the Egyptian pyramids.
> C   C   F   C   F F   C   C

The rest of this chapter will deal only with the various forms of content words. Later chapters will deal with function words (e.g., Chapt. 2. Articles, Chapt. 3. Pronouns, Chapt. 4. Aux-words) and with other aspects of content words (e.g., Chapt. 5. Verb Forms and Their Uses, Chapt. 6. Verbs and Time).

2. Content Words and Derivational Classes

2.1

There are four classes of content words:

Nouns	John, pencil, soap, air, mountain
Verbs	jump, think, read, go, remember
Adjectives	pretty, wild, hungry, blue, triangular
Adverbs	quickly, seriously, often, never, happily

A content word in one class usually has related forms in other classes. All these related forms make up a word family. Some word families have forms in all four classes. Others do not. Occasionally different forms of content words may be spelled the same way.

occasionally

Handwritten margin note:
Pronounce –
Archaeology
Occasionally
Gratitude
Gratify

2.2 Because all word families do not have forms in all classes, some words can be used only in certain sentence positions.

> A *grateful* (adjective) man may show his *gratitude* (noun) by thanking someone *gratefully* (adverb).

(In English there is no verb form in this *gratitude* word family. *Gratify* has a different meaning and does not express the idea of being grateful or showing gratitude. To show gratitude, we use another verb, *thank.*)

2.3 Sometimes there is more than one form in each class (see *circle* and *employ* in the list below). Sometimes the meanings of these different forms are very close (e.g., *circle* and *encircle*), but sometimes they are quite different (e.g., *employee, employer,* and *employment*).

Noun	Verb	Adjective	Adverb
beauty	beautify	beautiful	beautifully
vacancy	vacate	vacant	vacantly
jealousy	(no verb form)	jealous	jealously
qualification	qualify	qualified	(no adverb form)
work	work	working	(no adverb form)
circle	circle encircle	circular circled circling	circularly
employment employee employer	employ	employed employable	(no adverb form)

 A larger list of the forms of content words is found in Appendix A.

2.4 Some nouns and certain forms (*d-t-n* and *-ing*) of some verbs may be used as adjectives. (The use of verb forms in this way—traditionally called *participles*—is explained in Chapter 8.) When used as modifiers, they function as adjectives although they have noun or verb forms.

> The *working* man ate his *box* lunch.
> verb form   noun form
> adj. function   adj. function

Likewise, *-ing* verb forms may be used as nouns. (The use of these forms in this way—traditionally called gerunds—is explained in Chapter 13.) When used as subjects, objects, etc., these verb forms function like nouns.

> *Swimming* is fun, but I hate *running.*
> verb form   verb form
> noun function (subject)   noun function (object)

EXERCISE 2-A

Find the different forms of the following content words in the passage below. Underline or circle them. Then write all the different forms of these words in table or list form.

history	build	early	discover

ANCIENT AMERICAN RUINS

[1]No one knows the real history of the pyramids built in Mexico and Guatemala in earlier days, or who their builders were. [2]Many of these historic buildings were completely destroyed by the early Spaniards. [3]Christian churches were built on the sites of earlier Mayan and Toltec places of worship. [4]Historians state that later civilizations built upon the foundations of earlier buildings, even before the Spaniards came. [5]Many of the earlier discovered ruins have been rebuilt, and tourists come to see these historic buildings. [6]In Mexico City, workers, building a new subway, discovered unknown ruins from an earlier civilization. [7]When they started to build the Olympic Village, once again remnants of an early civilization were uncovered. [8]Historically, the discovery of any ancient ruin is a significant find, and historians and archaeologists are thrilled to discover one.

EXERCISE 2-B

Find the different forms of the following content words in the passage below. Underline or circle them. Then write all the different forms of these words in table or list form.

flower	tropical	beauty	produce	brief

FLOWERING TREES

[1]Flowering trees are often found in the tropics. [2]These trees produce beautiful flowers all year but do not bear edible fruit. [3]Their only valuable products are beauty and shade. [4]Their beautifully colored flowers are in contrast to the green that is seen everywhere in tropical climates.

[5]In other, nontropical parts of the world, the only flowers trees produce are blossoms, which beautify the environment just once a year. [6]The beauty of these blossoms lasts only a brief time but is often appreciated more because of its brevity. [7]This short period of beauty is often followed by another longer period of productivity during which fruit is produced.

EXERCISE 2-C

Find the different forms of the content words below in the following passage. Underline or circle them. Then write all the different forms of these words in table or list form.

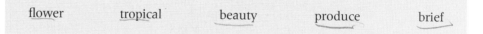

know	education	important	communicate

Know – Education – Important – Communicate.

FOREIGN LANGUAGE STUDY

¹The knowledge of a foreign language is an important part of an education. ²A person cannot be considered truly educated if he knows only one language. ³Nevertheless, the importance of learning foreign languages is often underestimated.

⁴English is one of the most commonly used languages in international communication. ⁵Some speakers of English mistakenly argue that it is unimportant for them to know another language for communicative purposes. ⁶They think that everyone else should know English. ⁷But there are still billions of people who do not speak English, and many of these people have limited educational opportunities. ⁸If English speakers do not make the effort to learn to communicate in other languages, they should not expect others to gain a knowledge of English.

⁹If there is to be world peace, the people of the world must understand each other. ¹⁰Communication is necessary to that understanding, but people cannot communicate if they do not speak the same language.

Inflectional – (Adj.)

3. Content Words and Inflectional Forms

3.1 All of the four classes of content words except the adverb class have a number of forms. Nouns may be singular or plural (this is explained in Chapter 2), each verb has six forms (this is explained in Chapter 5), and adjectives often have comparative and superlative forms (this is explained in Chapter 8).

Noun	Verb		Adjective	Adverb
anger (noncount)	anger angered angering	angers anger angered	angry angrier (the) angriest	angrily
civilization civilizations (count)	civilize civilized civilizing	civilizes civilize civilized	civilized (more) civilized (the most) civilized	(no adverb form)
kindness kindliness (noncount)	(no verb form)		kind	kindly
tolerance toleration (noncount)	tolerate tolerated tolerating	tolerates tolerate tolerated	tolerable (more) tolerable (the most) tolerable (more) tolerant (the most) tolerant	tolerably
action actions act acts actor actors actress actresses (count)	act acted acting	acts act acted	active (more) active (the most) active	actively
ability abilities (count and noncount)	enable enabled enabling	enables enable enabled	able abler (the) ablest	ably

3.2 You will notice in the preceding chart that the differences between the forms of each class are created by changes at the ends of the words. Other changes can be made at the front of some words by adding a prefix. However, the addition of a prefix changes the meaning of the word, and not the way it is used in a sentence.

Prefix	Meaning	Examples
pre-	(= before)	preview, prehistoric, preheat
re-	(= again)	replay, rewrite, redecorate
un-	(= negative)	unusual, unkind, unnatural

There are many prefixes in English. The ones above are only examples. Prefixes and their meanings can be found in a good dictionary.

Some prefixes have more than one meaning (e.g., *un-* used with a verb means a *reversal* of the action, not its *negative*). Sometimes one meaning is expressed by several different prefixes (e.g., *non-*, *un-*, *ir-*, *in-*, *im-*, and *mis-* all form the negative of the word they are added to). Words usually require a particular prefix for a meaning, and care must be taken to use the correct prefix. (For example, the prefix *im-* is the only negative prefix that can be used with the word *possible*. Similarly, if a negative meaning of the word *regular* is desired, only the prefix *ir-* can be added.)

EXERCISE 3-A

Find the different forms of the following content words in the passage below. Underline or circle them. Then write all the different forms of these words in table or list form. Label them NOUN, VERB, ADJ (adjective), or ADV (adverb). If a word's function is different from its form (see section 2.4 of this chapter), note both the form and the function.

history	discover	migrate	America

EARLY AMERICANS

[1]Historians would like to discover the origin of the American Indian, whose history is unknown. [2]Migration theories suggest origins in Asia, Egypt, or India. [3]Recorded history tells us that there were people living in America when Columbus discovered it. [4]Unlike the Polynesians, whose historical chants tell how their ancestors came in great canoes, the American Indians have no historical accounts of migration. [5]However, ruins built upon earlier ruins have been discovered which show that people did migrate to or within America. [6]The discovery of old buildings and artifacts sheds light on earlier civilizations and their migrations. [7]Historians continue to work with archaeologists to discover new facts about ancient American people and their migrations.

EXERCISE 3-B

Find the different forms of the content words below in the following passage. Underline or circle them. Then write all the different forms of these words in table or list form. Label them NOUN, VERB, ADJ (adjective), or ADV (adverb). If a word's function is different from its form (see section 2.4 of this chapter), note both the form and the function.

beautiful	art	paint

NOV. 16/94.   1:00 AM - Wednesday -

- Sentence construction -
① Content and function words -

In English there are two types of words?
   1- content words,
   2- function words.

Content words	Function words
book	a
diesel	the
archaeology	of
read	and
elephant	or
typewriter	not
quickly	when
horrible	about
man	under

The number of function words is very small (about 150) when compared with the large number of content words (hundreds of thousands and continually increasing).

ART

[1]Most of us appreciate art and admire a beautiful painting. [2]We wish we were artists and could paint a thing of beauty too. [3]What we fail to realize is the time the artist spends in preparation. [4]An artist spends hundreds of hours in art classes and invests hundreds of dollars in painting supplies before he can create a masterpiece. [5]Artistic talent is not enough; a talented person must develop his natural gift. [6]One is not a real artist until he has learned to make his brush and paints express artistically the beauty he sees around him.

[7]Writing is also an art. [8]Beautiful writing, like beautiful painting, involves an investment in time and energy. [9]Even talented writers must write and rewrite before their writing is artistically satisfying to both writer and reader.

EXERCISE 3-C   *Find the different forms of the following content words in the passage below. Underline or circle them. Then write all the different forms of these words in table or list form. Label them NOUN, VERB, ADJ (adjective), or ADV (adverb). If a word's function is different from its form (see section 2.4 of this chapter), note both the form and the function.*

tax	reduce	donate	deduct

TAXES

[1]Taxation is an inescapable part of modern life. [2]People must pay taxes on nearly everything. [3]They are taxed when they make money and taxed when they spend money. [4]They also pay taxes on things they own. [5]The federal government taxes people, and state and local governments also levy taxes. [6]People often do things to reduce their taxes. [7]To increase their deductions they make charitable donations, political contributions, and keep careful records of their deductible expenditures.

[8]Money donated to worthy causes benefits both the donor and the organization that receives the donation. [9]Many organizations depend on donors for much of their support, and donating money often reduces the taxpayer's taxable income, resulting in tax reductions.

[10]Sometimes people get in trouble by listing illegal deductions. [11]There are stiff penalties for tax evasion. [12]People should donate money to worthy causes and avoid paying more taxes than necessary, but they must not evade the payment of taxes they owe.

EXERCISE 3.1-A   *Here are some words. Write all the forms of each one in table form (as indicated). Remember, some words do not have all four forms. If a particular form does not exist, write Ø in that blank. Then fill in the blanks with the correct endings (noun, verb, adjective, and adverb forms) of the words whose beginnings are indicated.*

Noun	Verb	Adjective	Adverb
student	____	____	____
____	____	different	____
culture	____	____	____
____	____	____	friendly

CULTURE SHOCK

[1]When they go away to school, many *stud*_____ experience *cult*_____ shock. [2]The language is *diff*_____. [3]There are

other *diff*_____. [4]The food is cooked *diff*_____. [5]Every *cult*_____ has its own way of being *frie*_____—some are quiet, others are noisy. [6]A *stud*_____ misses family and *frie*_____ at home. [7]Although many students are very *stud*_____ and work hard, they can't *stud*_____ all the time. [8]As they become accustomed to the new *cult*_____, students experience less *cult*_____ shock. [9]When they make new *frie*_____, things don't seem as *diff*_____ as they used to. [10]Often when they return home, *stud*_____ have to adapt to *diff*_____ in their former *cult*_____ and once again suffer from *cult*_____ shock.

EXERCISE 3.1-B   *Here are some words. Write all the forms of each one in table form (as indicated). Remember, some words do not have all four forms. If a particular form does not exist, write Ø in that blank. Then fill in the blanks with the correct endings (noun, verb, adjective, and adverb forms) of the words whose beginnings are indicated.*

Noun	Verb	Adjective	Adverb
intelligence	_____	_____	_____
_____	compute	_____	_____
_____	_____	_____	capably
_____	_____	complex	_____
emotion	_____	_____	_____

COMPUTERS

[1]*Compu*_____ form an important part of our *compl*_____ modern civilization. [2]Our *compu*_____ world frightens some people. [3]They fear *compu*_____ because they think an "electronic brain" must be extremely *intel*_____. [4]Others reply that an "electronic brain" has no real *intel*_____; it can only *compu*_____. [5]Today, although *compu*_____ can beat champion chess players, they are not *intel*_____ or *emoti*_____. [6]They have no *intel*_____ or *emoti*_____, only memories. [7]*Compu*_____ are growing more and more *compl*_____. [8]As their *compl*_____ grow, so will their *capab*_____. [9]Someday *compu*_____ may be programmed to react *emoti*_____. [10]Then they may be *capab*_____ of human-like *emoti*_____. [11]Perhaps then *compu*_____ will have *emoti*_____ breakdowns as well as electronic ones.

EXERCISE 3.1-C   *Here are some words. Write all the forms of each one in table form (as indicated). Remember, some words do not have all four forms. If a particular form does not exist, write Ø in that blank. Then fill in the blanks with the correct endings (noun, verb, adjective, and adverb forms) of the words whose beginnings are indicated.*

Noun	Verb	Adjectives	Adverb
comfort	_____	_____	_____
_____	_____	foreign	_____
_____	notice	_____	_____
_____	_____	_____	strangely

CULTURAL ADJUSTMENT

[1]When people travel to *fore*_____ countries, they often do *stra*_____ things. [2]They don't realize that they, not the people around them, are the *fore*_____. [3]The *stra*_____ of their actions is not always *noti*_____ to them. [4]They don't understand why the local people look at them *stra*_____. [5]If they don't speak the local language, everything sounds *stra*_____ to them. [6]They begin to feel very un*comf*_____. [7]Frustrated by the *stra*_____ of the new environment, they retreat to the *comf*_____ of things from their own country. [8]They associate only with their fellow countrymen and *comf*_____ each other. [9]They avoid eating foods that are *noti*_____ different. [10]Sometimes they never become *comf*_____ with the local customs. [11]Then they return home impressed only by the *stra*_____ of people in *fore*_____ lands.

4. Proofreading

4.1 An important part of the process of writing is reading. Even the best writers make mistakes as they write. To ensure that their writing is correct, they have to go back and read (and re-read) what they have written to find and fix any mistakes. This is called *proofreading*.

Although you now have a better understanding of word types and forms, you may still make occasional mistakes with them. Therefore, like all other good writers, you also need to proofread your writing and correct your mistakes.

4.2 Proofreading is not easy. In fact, most people find it difficult to spot the mistakes in their own writing. It is often easier to find mistakes in someone else's writing than in your own. For this reason, you may want to exchange papers with a friend or classmate and proofread each other's writing when it is possible and permitted.

Another procedure that often helps people proofread better is to read their writing aloud. Reading aloud makes the mistakes more obvious and easier to spot. When possible, you should proofread by reading each word out loud—even if you have to do it quietly or "silently."

When you are proofreading, it is frequently a good idea to focus on a particular aspect of writing that you have difficulty with, such as subject-verb agreement, pronouns, spelling, or articles. Using this approach, you make several quick proofreading passes through a piece of writing, focusing on a particular area of difficulty each time.

The following exercises will give you practice in focused proofreading. The passages contain numerous mistakes with word types and forms, but that is the only type of error they contain. Using what you have learned in this chapter, focus on finding and fixing the incorrect forms of words.

EXERCISE 4-A

In the passage below, there are a number of word-form errors. Find them, correct them, and then rewrite the passage (or write your corrections on this page). Do not add any new words or take any away; just change the form of the existing words as necessary.

FLYING IN A SAILPLANE

[1]A sailplane is an aircraft that doesn't have an engine. [2]After being towed at the end of a longness towline by a car or other vehicle to a high of about 2,000 feet, the cable is released and the motorless sailplane glides through the air smooth and silence. [3]Under the right conditions, a sailplane can flight for a long time. [4]It can rise to great highnesses and cover amazing distants. [5]The world record for the highest altitude reached in a sailplane is 46,267 feet! [6]The world record for the longest distant flown in a sailplane is 647 miles!

[7]A sailplane has almost no instruments to watchful. [8]The pilot is left freedom to enjoy the feeling of gliding and soaring. [9]There is no noisy from the engine to disturb the peace and tranquil.

[10]In short, in a sailplane, you flight as man has always dreamed of flying. [11]Flying silently through the cloudy, you feel as freely as a bird, and what a thrill such free is! [12]Some people shout, song, or even cry for joyful the first time they go up in a sailplane.

EXERCISE 4-B

In the passage below, there are a number of word-form errors. Find them, correct them, and then rewrite the passage (or write your corrections on this page). Do not add any new words or take any away; just change the form of the existing words as necessary.

HANDLING ANGRY FEELINGS

[1]Abraham Lincoln once heard a friend who was speaking angry about someone. [2]Mr. Lincoln advice his friend to sit down and write all of his anger feelings in a letter. [3]"It will make you feel much better," said Lincoln.

[4]Lateness, when the letter was written, the friend read it to Lincoln, who commended it hearty for its severe. [5]The writer seemed happily and asked, "When would you advice me to send it?"

[6]"Send it?" responded Lincoln. [7]"Oh, I wouldn't send it. [8]I sometimes writing a letter like yours. [9]I find it makes me feel a lot better, but I never send it!"

[10]Nowadays, successful managers often follow a similar policy. [11]They usually have highly standards and are not always satisfaction with their employees. [12]One head of a famously hotel chain reports that handling such cases is a real

challenging for him. [13]He has a hard time controlling his angry. [14]Therefore, when an employment does something that makes him angrily, he uses an approach similar to Lincoln's. [15]He reports, "When I write a sharpness letter, I put it in the bottom drawer of my desk. [16]Then I wait a week and read it again. [17]If I still feel upsetting with the person, I send the letter, but usually I rip it up and throw it away."

EXERCISE 4-C   *In the passage below, there are a number of word-form errors. Find them, correct them, and then rewrite the passage (or write your corrections on this page). Do not add any new words or take any away; just change the form of the existing words as necessary.*

HOW TO GET FIRED

[1]In a recent study, a marketing researcher organization asked executives in one hundred of the nation's largeness companies what qualities in employees irritation bosses the most. [2]The respondents are revealing and can serve as a warn to any worker who may be slipping into trouble.

[3]At the top of the list of irritation qualities was dishonest. [4]If a company believes that an employee lacks integrity, all other positive qualities—from skillful and experience to productive and intelligent—become meaningless.

[5]Six other factors completion the list of "seven deadly sins" that can cause you to lost your job. [6]Here they are, arranged in order of irritating value, from the greatest to the least:

[7]Irresponsible. [8]If you goof off and do personal business on company time, you are asking for troubling.

[9]Arrogance. [10]Bosses don't like works who spend more time talking about their achieves than they do working.

[11]Absent and tardiness. [12]Bosses are not impressive with people who show up on the job lately—or not at all.

[13]Fail to follow instructions or company policy. [14]If an employee can't follow rules, management naturally feels he can't be trusted.

[15]Whining and complaining. [16]Some people are never satisfy with the assignments they are given or the conditions they worker in. [17]Is it any surprise that such people irritation their bosses?

[18]Lazy and lack of dedication. [19]If an employer doesn't care about the work he does or the firm he works for, he may end up looking for a newly job.

2

Nouns and Articles

This chapter will help you avoid or correct mistakes like these:

- I have too many homeworks tonight.
- These furnitures are beautiful.
- She has to buy some papers to write a letter.
- Prefixes and suffixes are the key to understanding English vocabularies.
- I need an information please.
- She has a pretty hair and a brown skin.
- In a modern civilization, the electricity is essential.
- _____ Modern world uses electricity all the time.
- We eat much meat and much vegetable_ every day.

1. Types of Nouns

English nouns are divided into two main groups: common and proper.

1.1   **Proper nouns** are the names of particular persons, places, or things. They are normally capitalized.

> George Washington
> Spain
> the Golden Gate Bridge

The rules for using articles with proper nouns are different from those for using articles with common nouns. Therefore, they will be discussed separately in section 7 of this chapter.

1.2   **Common nouns** may be countable or noncountable.

1.3   **Countable nouns** are plants, animals, objects with a definite shape, units of measurement, and many other things. Most countable nouns have singular and plural forms.

Singular	Plural
banana	bananas
gallon	gallons
hamburger	hamburgers
library	libraries
pencil	pencils

Some countable nouns (generally, the names of animals used for food) use the same form for both singular and plural.

Singular	Plural
sheep	sheep
deer	deer
fish	fish

A few countable nouns have no singular forms, only plural forms.

Singular	Plural
	people
	cattle

Some countable nouns are **group** or **collective nouns**.

> committee (a group of people who meet for a common purpose)
> faculty (the whole teaching staff at a school, **not** an individual teacher)
> herd (a group of animals, such as cattle, sheep, elephants)
> jury (a group of people who decide the verdict in a trial)
> team (a group of people who work or play together)

Group nouns are considered singular (and are followed by +s verb forms) when the entire group acts as a unit or is considered to be a single group. They are plural (and are followed by no -s verb forms) when each part acts individually.

> The jury has reached a verdict.
> The jury are arguing among themselves.
> The faculty is extremely well qualified at this school.
> The faculty are still debating the curriculum proposal.

1.4   **Noncountable nouns** do not have plural forms. They are followed by +s verb forms. (A list of common noncount nouns and their unit expressions is found in Appendix B of this book.)

Certain kinds of nouns are usually noncount:

Liquids, gases, metals:	water, oil, ink, oxygen, iron, silver
Substances made of many small particles:	sugar, rice, sand, snow
Materials used for building or making other things:	wood, cloth, paper, cardboard
Many types of food and drink:	bacon, bread, hamburger (ground beef), lettuce, lemonade, coffee, milk
Many abstract nouns and areas of study:	love, beauty, health, difficulty, intelligence, vision, geometry, biology

The noncount nouns that give learners of English the most difficulty, however, are those that do not fit into the above categories. In fact, many of them have meanings similar to those of count nouns.

Noncount	Count Noun Equivalents
mail	letters
homework	assignments
furniture	tables, chairs, etc.
advice	suggestions
baggage	suitcases
vocabulary	words

Remember that these are noncount nouns and should *not* be used in the plural (except when they are used to indicate different varieties, as explained in section 1.6).

> Incorrect: I have a lot of *homeworks* to do tonight.
> Correct: I have a lot of *homework* to do tonight.
>   I have a lot of *assignments* to do tonight.
>
> Incorrect: The *furnitures* in this room are very beautiful.
> Correct: The *furniture* in this room is very beautiful.
>   The *tables and chairs* in this room are very beautiful.

1.5 Some nouns can be either **count** or **noncount**. However, there is often an important difference between the count meaning and the noncount meaning.

> We bought *an iron*. (count noun, for ironing clothes)
> We bought *some iron*. (noncount noun, metal)

> Give me *a tape*. (count noun, a reel or cassette for a tape recorder)
> Give me *some tape*. (noncount noun, for sticking things together)

> She wants her *hamburger* without mustard. (count noun, grilled beef patty on a bun)
> She uses *hamburger* to make meat loaf. (noncount noun, ground beef)

> I saw *a film* at the Paramount Theater yesterday. (count noun, movie)
> I need *some film* for my camera. (noncount noun, for taking pictures)

> Kim has *a beautiful skin*. (count noun, hide of an animal)
> Kim has *beautiful skin*. (noncount noun, outer covering of the body)

> We need *a paper*. (count noun, newspaper)
> We need *some paper*. (noncount noun, material for writing on)

> I hate *gossip*. (noncount noun, idle talk, not always true, about other people)
> I hate *gossips*. (count noun, people who like to talk about others)

When you are not certain about the proper usage, it is wise to check a good dictionary that distinguishes between count meanings (often indicated with a [C]) and noncount/uncountable meanings (often indicated with a [U]).

1.6 Noncount nouns may become count nouns when they are used to indicate classes, species, varieties, or kinds.

> The *foods* of Hawaii (pineapple, poi, taro, breadfruit, etc.) seem very exotic to tourists who visit the islands.
> The doctor told me I should do *more exercise*. (greater amount)
> The doctor told me I should do *more exercises*. (greater variety)

1.7 When asking or answering questions about quantity, you must know if the noun is a count or noncount noun and then use the appropriate question expression. *How many* is used with count nouns. *How much* is used with noncount nouns.

> How *many bananas* do you want? (count noun)
> How *much rice* do you want? (noncount noun)
> How *many suitcases* do you have? (count noun)
> How *much baggage* do you have? (noncount noun)

1.8 General, indefinite expressions of quantity or amount also vary depending on whether the noun they are used with is count or noncount.

	Count Noun	**Noncount Noun**
For a **small** amount	*a few** *few*	*a little** *little*
For a **large** amount	*many* *a lot of* *lots of* (informal)	*much* *a lot of* *lots of* (informal)

*For guidance about when to use the article *a* with *few* and *little*, see section 6 in this chapter.

> There are *many* bananas on the table. (count noun)
> There is *a lot of* rice in that bag. (noncount noun)
> We have *a lot of* things to do today. (count noun)
> We have *much* work to do today. (noncount noun)
> I have only *a few* suitcases. (count noun)
> I have only *a little* baggage. (noncount noun)

EXERCISE 1-A *In the following passage, the nouns have been italicized. Write a C above each count noun, and write NC above each noncount noun.*

PARTY PREPARATIONS

[1]Preparing for the *party*, Sarah took a lot of *time* to get dressed. [2]First she took a relaxing *bath* with special *oil* in the *water*. [3]Then she put on her *clothing*, including her new *skirt* and favorite *blouse*. [4]Next she brushed her *hair*. [5]When she finished, she was careful to clean off any *hairs* that had fallen on her *clothes*. [6]After that, she brushed her *teeth*. [7]She used a new kind of *toothpaste* she had bought earlier that day. [8]Next came her *makeup*. [9]She used her normal *lipstick* and *eye shadow* but tried a new *perfume*. [10]Finally, she put on her *jewelry*—a gold *bracelet* and *necklace* and a pair of diamond *earrings*. [11]At last, she was ready for her special *evening*.

EXERCISE 1-B   *In the following passage, the nouns have been italicized. Write a C above each count noun, and write NC above each noncount noun.*

LOSING WEIGHT

[1]I need to lose some *weight*. [2]I can't decide whether to cut down on the *food* I eat or increase the *amount* of *exercise* I do. [3]Maybe I'll do both, but it will take a lot of *will power*. [4]I love fattening *foods* with lots of *sugar* and *calories* and I hate *exercises* like *sit ups*. [5]In fact, even the *thought* of *exercise* makes me tired. [6]Perhaps it would be best to go to the shopping *mall* and buy myself a new *wardrobe*. [7]I really enjoy shopping for *clothing*. [8]Of course, that would take a lot of *money*, and I have only a few *dollars* left to last me until the *end* of the *month*. [9]Maybe I'll just avoid looking at myself in *mirrors*.

EXERCISE 1-C   *In the following passage, the nouns have been italicized. Write a C above each count noun, and write NC above each noncount noun.*

HOMEWORK BLUES

[1]I have a *ton* of *homework* to do tonight. [2]I can't believe how my *assignments* are piling up. [3]The *teachers* must conspire to make all the big *projects* due on the same *day*. [4](That's just my *luck* to attend a *school* with a sadistic *faculty*.) [5]Getting everything done by tomorrow will be a great *test* of my *intelligence* and *determination*. [6]Then, of course, there will be more *work* to do for the following *day*. [7]I'll be lucky to get through this *semester* with my *health* and *GPA* (*grade point average*) intact. [8]On top of everything else, my *supplies* are running out. [9]Will you lend me some *paper* so I can start writing my history *paper*?

EXERCISE 1.1-A   *Write* How much *or* How many, *whichever is appropriate, in the blanks.*

THIS CLASS

1. _____ students are there in this class?
2. _____ homework do you have to do?
3. _____ books do you need to buy?
4. _____ money do they cost?
5. _____ time do you have to spend studying every day?
6. _____ tests are there?
7. _____ students attend this school?
8. _____ nationalities do they represent?
9. _____ languages do they speak?
10. _____ tuition do they have to pay?
11. _____ material do they study?
12. _____ things do they learn?

EXERCISE 1.1-B   *Write* How much *or* How many, *whichever is appropriate, in the blanks.*

YOUR CAR

1. _____ money did you pay for this car?

2. _____ years have you owned it?

3. _____ miles have you driven it?

4. _____ gas is in the gas tank?

5. _____ miles per gallon do you get?

6. _____ cylinders does it have?

7. _____ carburetors does it have?

8. _____ power does it have?

9. _____ water did you put in the radiator?

10. _____ oil do you have to add every week?

11. _____ air pressure does each tire take?

12. _____ tread is left on each one?

EXERCISE 1.1-C   *Write* How much *or* How many, *whichever is appropriate, in the blanks.*

THE NEWS

1. _____ news was there on the TV today?

2. _____ people listened to it?

3. _____ sports coverage was there?

4. _____ minutes did the entire broadcast take?

5. _____ emphasis was given to the weather?

6. _____ advertisements were there?

7. _____ different sponsors were there?

8. _____ local broadcasters appeared?

9. _____ men were on the news team?

10. _____ women were there?

11. _____ national news was there?

12. _____ time did you waste watching TV today?

EXERCISE 1.2-A   *Fill in the blanks with* a few, a little, much, many, *or* a lot of, *whichever is appropriate.*

SUMMER CAMP

[1]I am really enjoying my vacation here at Camp Lottafun. [2]There are

_____ things to do. [3]In fact, there are so _____

possible activities that I can't do them all. [4]I am, however, getting

_____ exercise and having _____ fun trying.

⁵For example, there is a large lake stocked with _____ kinds of game fish. ⁶You can catch them from shore, or you can go out on the lake in a canoe. ⁷There are _____ of them at the boathouse so you don't even have to wait. ⁸If you don't like canoes, there are even _____ rowboats, but not very _____. ⁹They are not as popular as the canoes.

¹⁰I have also made _____ new friends. ¹¹Because there are so _____, I can't name them all. ¹²There must be over a hundred! ¹³_____, however, are special. ¹⁴I will miss them the most when camp is over. ¹⁵We have enjoyed _____ memorable times together, and my journal is full of stories about the _____ fun adventures we have shared.

¹⁶Well, other than that, there is not _____ news to report. ¹⁷I'll see you when I get back home next week.

EXERCISE 1.2-B   *Fill in the blanks with* a few, a little, much, many, *or* a lot of, *whichever is appropriate.*

CLASSMATES

¹At my school there are _____ different types of students. ²Studying them adds _____ variety to my boring routine.

³There are _____ "nerds." ⁴They are the "brains" of the school, but they don't have _____ social skills. ⁵They know _____ geometry and chemistry, but they can't quite comprehend modern fashions. ⁶I'm glad there are only _____ of them.

⁷In contrast, there are also _____ "jocks." ⁸They are the athletes, or those who think they are athletic. ⁹There are hundreds of them! ¹⁰They try to look "cool" by wearing athletic shoes and clothes. ¹¹They must spend _____ money on them, but that doesn't mean they are real athletes. ¹²I know that only _____ of them are on our school teams.

¹³Of course, there are also _____ "fashion plates." ¹⁴Their biggest concern in life is how they look. ¹⁵They wear the most fashionable clothes, _____ jewelry, and _____ makeup. ¹⁶They spend _____ hours fixing their hair so it has the right "natural" look.

¹⁷And then, there are the "normal" students. ¹⁸Unfortunately, there are only _____ of us left. ¹⁹I guess we are a vanishing species.

EXERCISE 1.2-C   *Fill in the blanks with* a few, a little, much, many, *or* a lot of, *whichever is appropriate.*

HOBBIES

¹_____ people have hobbies. ²They are a common way to spend extra time and get _____ more enjoyment out of life.

³Cooking is a popular hobby. ⁴For _____ people, cooking is not a chore but a fun activity which offers _____ adventure. ⁵There are _____ challenges involved in preparing a new dish. ⁶It is important to follow the recipe carefully. ⁷Too _____ salt or too _____ drops of vanilla extract can ruin the taste. ⁸When they succeed, however, cooks get _____ emotional, as well as gastronomical, rewards.

⁹Another popular hobby is sewing. ¹⁰Nowadays (compared with fifty years ago), not as _____ people sew, but there are still quite _____ "seamsters" around. ¹¹They are not all professional tailors or seamstresses, but they sew because it gives them _____ pleasure to create something out of fabric. ¹²Some of them use _____ material for large projects, and some use only _____ scraps to make doll clothes.

¹³There are _____ more hobbies I could write about. ¹⁴As I think about it, the list seems endless. ¹⁵Nevertheless, these examples illustrate how people can get _____ pleasure from what other people consider to be work.

2. Noncount Nouns and Unit Expressions

2.1   Count nouns indicate units. To indicate quantity, all that is necessary is a number before the noun.

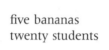

> five bananas
> twenty students

Unit expressions of quantity may also be used with count nouns.

> five boxes of pencils
> two crates of oranges

2.2   Noncount nouns do not indicate units. When referring to quantity, noncount nouns require a unit expression. When you learn a noncount noun, you should also learn the appropriate unit expressions that go with it. (Appendix B lists some common noncount nouns and unit expressions.) The number is placed before the unit expression.

> five bowls of rice
> three rooms of furniture

When quantity is not being considered (that is, the meaning is generic [see section 3 in this chapter]), the unit expression is not necessary.

> Furniture is expensive.
> Butter contains vitamin A.

EXERCISE 2

The nouns listed below are all noncount nouns. Use appropriate unit expressions in answering the question "What did you buy when you went to the supermarket?"

> soap (3)   I bought three bars of soap.
> milk (2)   I bought two cartons of milk.
> butter (1) I bought a pound of butter.

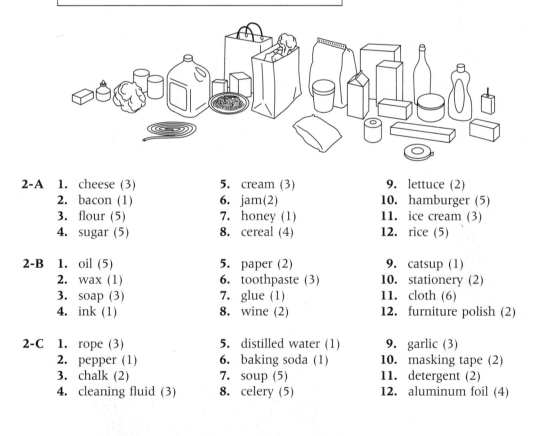

2-A	1. cheese (3)	5. cream (3)	9. lettuce (2)
	2. bacon (1)	6. jam (2)	10. hamburger (5)
	3. flour (5)	7. honey (1)	11. ice cream (3)
	4. sugar (5)	8. cereal (4)	12. rice (5)
2-B	1. oil (5)	5. paper (2)	9. catsup (1)
	2. wax (1)	6. toothpaste (3)	10. stationery (2)
	3. soap (3)	7. glue (1)	11. cloth (6)
	4. ink (1)	8. wine (2)	12. furniture polish (2)
2-C	1. rope (3)	5. distilled water (1)	9. garlic (3)
	2. pepper (1)	6. baking soda (1)	10. masking tape (2)
	3. chalk (2)	7. soup (5)	11. detergent (2)
	4. cleaning fluid (3)	8. celery (5)	12. aluminum foil (4)

3. Articles and Nouns—Generic

3.1   Besides being countable or noncountable, English nouns have other dimensions. They may be generic or nongeneric in meaning. If they are nongeneric, they may be definite (specifically identified) or indefinite. Articles (*a/an, the*) and other determiners (*some*) indicate these dimensions of English nouns.

3.2   Sometimes a noun is used to represent an entire group or class, in general. It does not refer to a specific thing but rather serves as a symbol for the whole group. To indicate this **generic** meaning for countable nouns, the **plural** form of the noun is usually used with **no article**.

> *Horses* are beautiful animals. (meaning: all horses, in general)
> *Bananas* are my favorite fruit. (meaning: all bananas, in general)
> *People* are the most intelligent creatures on earth. (meaning: all human beings, in general)

3.3   Sometimes, however, the **singular** form is used with the article *a/an* or *the* to indicate this generic meaning.

> *The honeybee* is an insect that many people admire.
> *A chair* can be used for many purposes.
> *An apple* is usually red, but it can also be green or yellow.

3.4   With a few countable nouns, it is possible to use the **singular** form **without any article** at all to indicate generic meaning.

> *Man* is the most intelligent creature on earth. (meaning: all human beings, in general)

3.5   **Noncountable** nouns have only one form (no singular or plural). To indicate the generic meaning of a noncountable noun, it is used **without any article or determiner**.

> *Fuel* comes in various forms. (meaning: fuel in general)
> *Gold* is a very precious metal. (meaning: gold in general)

3.6   Certain adjectives are sometimes used to represent the noun group they modify. In such cases, the noun is not used, but the article *the* is.

> Robin Hood robbed *rich people* and gave money to *poor people*.
> Robin Hood robbed *the rich* and gave money to *the poor*.
>
> *The English navy* defeated *the Spanish armada*.
> *The English* defeated *the Spanish*.
>
> *Elderly people* often need help from *young people*.
> *The elderly* often need help from *the young*.
>
> *That which is unknown* frightens most people.
> *The unknown* frightens most people.

4. Articles and Nouns—Indefinite

4.1   Most often, nouns are used in their nongeneric sense. They do not refer to an entire group or class in general but to an actual, specific thing. When a nongeneric noun is not specifically identified, it is called "indefinite."

4.2   With **singular, countable nouns**, this indefinite meaning is indicated by the use of the article *a/an*.

> I need *an* onion. (meaning: no specific onion, any onion will do)
> Let's buy *a* new clock. (meaning: we have not yet decided which clock to buy)

The *an* form is used before words beginning with vowel sounds, and the *a* form is used before words beginning with consonant sounds. Remember that it is the *sound* (not the spelling) that matters.

> *an* hour (the *h* is "silent")
> *an* honest man (the *h* is "silent")
> *a* university (begins with a *y* sound)

4.3   With **plural, countable nouns,** this indefinite meaning is indicated by the use of the determiner *some* (or a determiner that indicates number, such as *two* or *several*).

> I would like to plant *some* flowers in our yard. (meaning: any flowers)
> *Some* men came in here and started shouting. (the men are not indentified)
> *Several* books have been stolen. (we don't yet know which ones)

4.4   With **noncountable nouns**, this indefinite meaning is indicated by the use of the determiner *some* also.

> We need to buy *some* gasoline soon.
> After years of prospecting, they finally found *some* gold.

EXERCISE 4-A   *Write* a, an, *or* some, *whichever is appropriate, in the blanks.*

LUNCHTIME

¹Would you like _____ orange? ²No, but I would like _____ orange juice. ³I'm sorry. We don't have any orange juice. Would you like _____ coffee? ⁴No thank you. I'll just have _____ sandwich. ⁵Would you like _____ tomato juice to go with it? ⁶No, I just had _____ tomato soup. ⁷How about _____ egg? ⁸That sounds good, but I think I'll have _____

hot dog instead. [9]After that I want to eat _____ banana or two. [10]I might have _____ milk with the bananas. [11]I would like _____ other fruit also, but I can't see any. [12]To finish off, I will have _____ tea. [13]I'd like _____ sugar in it, but not too much. [14]That was _____ delicious lunch. [15]I need only one more thing, _____ toothpick.

EXERCISE 4-B   *Write* a, an, *or* some, *whichever is appropriate, in the blanks.*

FRIENDS

[1]Everyone needs _____ friend. [2]_____ true friend is _____ person who remains _____ friend even when _____ problem arises. [3]_____ people are "fair weather" friends who always want to share _____ good time but are not to be found when _____ unpleasant situation occurs. [4]_____ people are friends with anyone who has _____ money or has _____ power or influence. [5]Are you _____ true friend or, like _____ others, _____ "fair weather" friend?

EXERCISE 4-C   *Write* a, an, *or* some, *whichever is appropriate, in the blanks.*

GAINING KNOWLEDGE

[1]_____ students feel they need _____ reason to read _____ book. [2]Unless _____ teacher gives _____ assignment to read _____ specific chapter, the students do not look at even _____ page of the text. [3]Although _____ instruction is given orally, unless _____ student does _____ reading from the text and _____ research in outside sources, he will have _____ knowledge of the subject, but it will be limited. [4]_____ true scholar always seeks _____ additional knowledge on _____ subject. [5]He thus has _____ better understanding of the subject than _____ of the other students.

5. Articles and Nouns—Definite

5.1   Nongeneric nouns may become "definite" or specifically identified in several ways:

1. By being mentioned in a previous sentence.

> There was once *a* little boy. *The* boy lived in *a* small house. *The* house was made of candy.

2. By identifying information given later in the same sentence.

> *The* trophy on the shelf is mine.

3. By the situation.

> When I got out of bed this morning, I opened *the* window.
>   (The window is in my bedroom.)
> The teacher told George to put his gum in *the* wastebasket.
>   (There is only one wastebasket in the classroom.)

5.2   The article *the* is used when a noun is "definite" (specifically identified). It does not matter whether the noun is noncountable or countable, singular or plural. Other determiners (possessives, such as *my* and *your*, or demonstratives, such as *this* and *those*) may also be used with definite nouns.

> *The* pirate found *the* gold he had buried years earlier.
> *The* clock we bought has a one-year warranty.
> *The* flowers in *your* yard look very pretty.
> *Those* desks are very old.

This test may help you decide whether to use *a/an* or *the* before a noun. Ask the question, "Which _____ (insert the noun)?" If you have enough information to answer it in a way that distinguishes this noun from all others, then it is probably identified, and you should use the article *the*.

> We saw *a* nice refrigerator in the store, but it was very expensive. (This is the first mention, and the refrigerator is not yet identified, so the article used is *a*.)
>
> We decided to save our money and buy *the* refrigerator as soon as we could. ("Which refrigerator?" The expensive one we saw in the store. The refrigerator is now identified, so the article used is *the*.)

5.3   The chart below summarizes the preceding presentation of the various types of English nouns and the articles that go with them.

English Nouns and Articles

	Count		Noncount
	Singular	**Plural**	
Generic	An apple The apple A chair The chair	Apples Chairs	Fruit Furniture
Indefinite	An apple A chair	Some apples Some chairs	Some fruit Some furniture
Definite	The apple The chair	The apples The chairs	The fruit The furniture

EXERCISE 5-A *Write* a, an, *or* the, *whichever is appropriate, in the blanks.*

A TRAFFIC INCIDENT

[1]I saw _____ boy walking across the street today. [2]_____ boy was almost hit by _____ car. [3]_____ car was speeding. [4]_____ policeman saw what happened. [5]_____ policeman chased and stopped _____ car. [6]He gave _____ driver of _____ car _____ ticket. [7]_____ ticket cost _____ speeding motorist forty-five dollars.

EXERCISE 5-B *Write* a, an, *or* the, *whichever is appropriate, in the blanks.*

THE LION AND THE MOUSE

[1]_____ lion was awakened by _____ mouse running across his face. [2]With _____ great roar, _____ lion grabbed _____ mouse and was about to kill him. [3]"Oh please," _____ mouse begged. "Spare my life! Someday I will repay your kindness." [4]_____ lion was so amused at _____ thought of _____ small mouse being able to help _____ king of beasts that he let _____ tiny creature go. [5]Later _____ lion, caught in _____ trap set by some hunters, was hopelessly tangled in _____ net of strong ropes. [6]_____ lion roared so loudly that all _____ beasts in _____ forest heard him. [7]_____ mouse recognized _____ roar and ran to _____ place where _____ lion lay trapped. [8]_____ mouse began to chew _____ rope until at last _____ lion was free. [9]"Thank you," said _____ lion. [10]"I now see that _____ weak can help _____ strong."

EXERCISE 5-C *Write* a, an, *or* the, *whichever is appropriate, in the blanks.*

THE LION AND THE DONKEY

[1]_____ donkey and _____ rooster lived together in _____ farmyard. [2]One day _____ hungry lion passed by. [3]When he saw _____ plump donkey, he thought of _____ fine meal it would make. [4]Just as _____ lion was about to pounce on _____ donkey, _____ rooster began to crow. [5]Now there is nothing _____ lion hates more than _____ sound of _____ rooster's crowing. [6]_____ lion turned and ran away at _____ sound of _____ *cock-a-doodle-doo.* [7]_____ donkey laughed. [8]"Look, _____ lion is _____ coward! [9]_____ mighty king of beasts runs from _____ rooster." [10]Then _____ donkey felt so bold that he began to chase _____ lion. [11]He had not run very far, however, when _____ lion turned and leaped upon _____ donkey. [12]_____ rooster, watching from _____ farmyard, said sadly, "It's too bad my poor friend did not understand what he could and could not do."

EXERCISE 5.1-A *Write* a, an, *or* the, *whichever is appropriate, in the blanks.*

A STAGECOACH RIDE—PART I

[1]In _____ first half of _____ 1800s, _____ best way to travel from _____ eastern United States to California was on _____ stagecoach. [2]Missouri was where _____ railroad ended and horses took over. [3]From there, _____ trip west was often _____ exciting adventure.

[4]Starting at _____ end of _____ line, passengers had to get to _____ stage station at dawn and wait in line for _____ ticket and _____ seat. [5]_____ ticket gave its owner _____ right to fifteen inches of seat space, perhaps with _____ fat man on one side and _____ scared woman on _____ other. [6]Those who were not first aboard often found themselves sitting on _____ hard jump seat. [7]This was _____ seat on _____ side of _____ coach. [8] It had no back and was very uncomfortable.

[9]When it was time to leave, _____ driver would climb up on his seat in front of _____ coach. [10]Spitting _____ tobacco juice from his mouth, he would call out "All aboard!" and release _____ brakes with _____ jerk. [11]Making _____ loud crack with his whip, he got _____ six-horse team off to _____ fast start.

EXERCISE 5.1-B *Write* a, an, *or* the, *whichever is appropriate, in the blanks.*

A STAGECOACH RIDE—PART II

[1]_____ good driver directed _____ team of horses with gentle tugs on _____ reins. [2]As one experienced stage driver once told _____ small boy, "Son, I talk to them through _____ ribbons."

[3]Quickly, _____ main street of _____ town where _____ stage started was left behind. [4]As they rode across _____ prairie, passengers saw wild game everywhere, and they also passed lone hunters, settlers' homes, and Indian families.

[5]After covering about twelve miles, _____ stage they were in would reach _____ "swing" station. [6]While _____ passengers got out to "stretch their

legs," _____ stock handlers at _____ station quickly changed _____ horses. [7]Then, _____ stage and its passengers were off again.

[8]After about fifty miles, they would come to _____ "home station" operated by _____ stationmaster and his family. [9]_____ home station served hot meals for _____ passengers. [10]They would also sleep at _____ home station nearest to where _____ stage was at _____ end of _____ day since most stages stopped at night. [11]It was hard for drivers to see in _____ dark, and _____ horses might bolt at _____ sight of _____ huge tumbleweed blowing across _____ road in front of them at night.

EXERCISE 5.1-C   *Write* a, an, *or* the, *whichever is appropriate, in the blanks.*

A STAGECOACH RIDE—PART III

[1]Because stagecoaches often carried large amounts of gold dust and money, they were often stopped by highway robbers. [2]These hold ups were always frightening, but not always dangerous to _____ passengers. [3]In one hold up, for instance, _____ frightened woman threw her purse out of _____ coach when _____ stage she was riding in was held up by _____ gang of robbers. [4]To her surprise, _____ robber threw her bag back to her saying, "Lady, we don't want your money; we only want Wells Fargo's."

[5]_____ usual length of time for _____ journey from Kansas to San Francisco was eighteen days. [6]However, for _____ sake of publicity, Ben Holladay, _____ owner of _____ Overland Stage Company, once made _____ exciting dash from San Francisco to Kansas in just twelve days. [7]Newspaper headlines proclaimed him "The King of Hurry." [8]Of course, today _____ modern jet can cover _____ same distance in just _____ few hours.

[9]Before airplanes crossed the country, however, trains did. [10]In 1869 _____ Union Pacific and Central Pacific railroads finally met in Utah. [11]In _____ ceremony which was held to celebrate _____ placing of _____ last rail and _____ joining of East and West, _____ golden spike was hammered into place. [12]It marked _____ beginning of _____ new era in U.S. transportation but _____ death of _____ stagecoach. [13]Passengers naturally preferred to cross _____ country in _____ comfortable, speedy train, and soon _____ stagecoach became _____ relic of history to be seen only in Western movies and television shows.

6. Expressions of Quantity with *a*

6.1 Some expressions of quantity use *a* although they are used with noncount nouns or plural count nouns (which are never used with *a* alone).

a few (count noun plural)	*A few* students came to the meeting.
a little (noncount noun)	Just use *a little* sugar.
a great many (count noun plural)	*A great many* people came to the meeting.
a couple of (count noun plural)	I'll be ready in *a couple of* minutes.
a lot of (either noncount or count noun plural)	*A lot of* time is needed to get it ready. *A lot of* people are needed for this play.
a number of (count noun plural)	*A number of* people are waiting to see you.

6.2 The meanings of the phrases *a few* and *a little* are different from the meanings of the single words *few* and *little*. This difference lies in the emphasis or point of view of the writer or speaker.

> *A few* people came to the meeting. (Positive meaning—at least somebody came)
> *Few* people came to the meeting. (Negative meaning—not as many as expected)
> There's *a little hope* for the injured boy. (Positive meaning—he may live)
> There's *little hope* for the injured boy. (Negative meaning—he'll probably die)

EXERCISE 6-A *In the sentences below, the meaning changes depending on whether the article* a *is used. Read each sentence and the one that follows it. After you have determined the correct meaning, write the article* a *or the symbol* ∅ *(no article) in the blank provided.*

1. _____ few people came to the meeting. I was very disappointed.

2. _____ few people came to the meeting. Therefore, we went ahead with it.

3. There is _____ little jam left in the jar. You can probably make one more sandwich.

4. There is _____ little jam left in the jar. Why don't you throw it away?

5. I have _____ little hope for you. You will probably fail.

6. I have _____ little hope for you. You may succeed.

7. There were _____ few cherries on the trees. We climbed up and picked all that we could.

8. There were _____ few cherries on the trees. We didn't go to the trouble of climbing up to pick them.

9. There is _____ little orange juice left for breakfast. I'll have to make some more.

10. There is _____ little milk. Let's drink that instead.

EXERCISE 6-B

In the sentences below, the meaning changes depending on whether the article a *is used. Read each sentence and the one that follows it. After you have determined the correct meaning, write the article* a *or the symbol* ∅ *(no article) in the blank provided.*

1. He has given _____ little thought to the problem or its solution. He needs more time to think about it.

2. He has given _____ little thought to the problem. Maybe he can suggest a solution.

3. He has _____ little money in the bank. Let's help by giving him some of ours.

4. He has _____ little money in the bank. Let him withdraw it and help himself.

5. There is _____ little wood in the Arctic. People there depend on other materials for fuel and shelter.

6. There is _____ little wood in the desert. Although the people there must be very frugal with it, they use wood for tools, homes, and fuel.

7. Professor Jones does _____ little research. He should reserve time for it.

8. Professor Smith does _____ little research. He does what he can at night and on weekends.

9. There are _____ few opportunities for advancement in this company. I should look for a new employer.

10. There are _____ few opportunities for advancement in this company. I'll work hard and try for a promotion.

EXERCISE 6-C

In the sentences below, the meaning changes depending on whether the article a *is used. Read each sentence and the one that follows it. After you have determined the correct meaning, write the article* a *or the symbol* ∅ *(no article) in the blank provided.*

1. There were _____ few leaves on the ground. Nevertheless, the gardener raked them up anyway.

2. There were _____ leaves on the ground. The gardener obviously hadn't done a very good job.

3. George put _____ little effort into his work. He was surprised to find he could succeed.

4. George put _____ little effort into his work. No wonder he was not successful.

5. Jack found _____ little peanut butter in the jar. At least it was enough for one sandwich.

6. Contrary to what he expected, Jack found _____ little peanut butter in the jar. It wasn't enough to make even one sandwich.

7. It was April and _____ few tulips could be seen in the garden. Marge knew that the long winter was almost over.

8. It was April and _____ few tulips could be seen in the garden. Marge wondered if the long winter would ever end.

9. I have _____ little money. I doubt that it's enough for a ticket.

10. I have _____ little money. Let's see if it is enough for a ticket.

7. Articles and Proper Nouns

7.1 *The* is the only article used with proper nouns (the names of people, places, institutions, etc.) and it is not used with all proper nouns. It is used only in certain cases as explained below.

7.2 The article *the* is usually used...

1. when *of* is part of the name.

> the United States of America   the Bank of America
> the University of Michigan   (an exception is Lloyds of London)
> the Bay of Biscay

2. with the names of...

oceans	the Pacific Ocean
canals	the Panama Canal
rivers	the Hudson River
seas	the Dead Sea
channels	the English Channel
gulfs	the Gulf of Mexico
deserts	the Gobi Desert
peninsulas	the Iberian Peninsula
forests	the Black Forest
freeways	the Riverside Expressway
turnpikes	the Pennsylvania Turnpike
bridges	the Golden Gate Bridge
libraries	the Carnegie Library
museums	the Metropolitan Museum
other buildings	the Empire State Building
clubs	the Rotary Club
documents	the Mayflower Compact

3. with the **plural** names of...

islands	the Aleutian Islands
lakes	the Great Lakes
mountains (mountain ranges)	the Rocky Mountains
continents	the Americas
countries	the Philippines

4. with the names of distinct geographic areas employing the points of the compass (i.e., north, east, etc.)

> the South
> the Pacific Northwest

7.3   The article *the* is usually **not** used . . .

1. when a possessive noun is part of the name.

> St. Peter's Cathedral
> Harrah's Club

2. with the names of . . .

planets **beaches** **bays** **passes**	Mars Omaha Beach Hudson Bay Donner Pass
parks **stadiums**	Golden Gate Park Yankee Stadium
streets **avenues** **boulevards** **roads** **lanes**	Main Street Pennsylvania Avenue Ventura Boulevard Canyon Road Sunnybrook Lane
states and provinces	Virginia, Alberta
universities and colleges (unless *of* is part of the name)	Harvard University

3. with the *singular* names of . . .

islands **lakes** **bays** **mountains** **continents** **countries** (unless *of* is part of the name) **cities**	Pitcairn Island Lake Victoria Manila Bay Mount Rushmore Africa Japan Chicago

7.4   Even with the help of the above rules, the use of the article *the* is not always predictable. Some proper nouns use the article while others that seem very similar (in meaning or form) do not. Compare the following examples:

without *the*	with *the*
Russia North Africa Death Valley	the Soviet Union the North Pole the San Joaquin Valley

EXERCISE 7-A   *Write articles (a, an, or the) in the blanks when needed. If no article is necessary, write the symbol ∅.*

A SHORT VACATION

[1]Many people like to travel on holiday _____ weekends. [2]Driving their own _____ cars, they can go as far as they want and stop when they please. [3]_____ nice three- or four-day trip from _____ Los Angeles, California, is to drive up to _____ San Francisco either following _____ Pacific Ocean Highway or alternately through _____ San Joaquin Valley. [4]_____ nice

side trip from _____ San Francisco is to cross _____ Golden Gate Bridge and drive through _____ redwood forests of _____ Northern California. [5]After _____ return through _____ Sacramento, one can drive by _____ Lake Tahoe and over _____ Donner Pass through _____ Sierra Nevada Mountains. [6]After passing through _____ Reno, _____ route goes through _____ Mojave Desert. [7]If it's _____ summer trip, one should avoid _____ Death Valley and come back over _____ mountains through _____ pass in _____ Sierra Nevadas, crossing _____ California–Nevada border near _____ Baker, California. [8]_____ delightful drive paralleling _____ Los Angeles aqueduct is part of _____ return trip to _____ Los Angeles.

EXERCISE 7-B   *Write articles (a, an, or the) in the blanks when needed. If no article is necessary, write the symbol ∅.*

A QUICK TRIP AROUND THE WORLD—PART I

[1]_____ international airline advertises that one can take _____ trip around _____ world in _____ three days. [2]Some people have actually made this three-day trip. [3]Leaving at _____ Los Angeles, it consists of crossing _____ Pacific Ocean to _____ Japan with _____ short stop on _____ island of Oahu in _____ Hawaii. [4]This stop is not long enough to visit _____ Waikiki Beach or even see _____ palm tree. [5]After this brief stop, _____ flight is again over _____ Pacific Ocean without _____ stop in _____ Philippines or on any of _____ islands in _____ Micronesia. [6]One cannot stay in _____ Tokyo for _____ night's rest or to see famous _____ Mt. Fuji. [7]After _____ flight over _____ Taiwan, _____ Hong Kong is _____ next stop. [8]Then it's over _____ Yellow Sea, seeing _____ Macao and _____ Vietnam only from _____ air. [9]There is _____ short stop in _____ New Delhi (which is in _____ India), but there is not time to visit _____ Taj Mahal in _____ Agra. [10]Then it's on to _____ Beirut for _____ twenty-minute stop and from there to _____ Rome, Italy. [11]One can only dream of seeing _____ Vatican, _____ Sistine Chapel, _____ St. Peter's Cathedral, and all _____ other beautiful sights in _____ Italy as _____ plane is soon on its way to _____ Paris, France. [12]Along the way, if it's _____ clear day, one can see _____ Alps in all their snowy splendor. [13]In _____ Paris, unfortunately, there is no _____ time to see _____ Eiffel Tower and _____ Louvre—probably _____ most famous museum in _____ world.

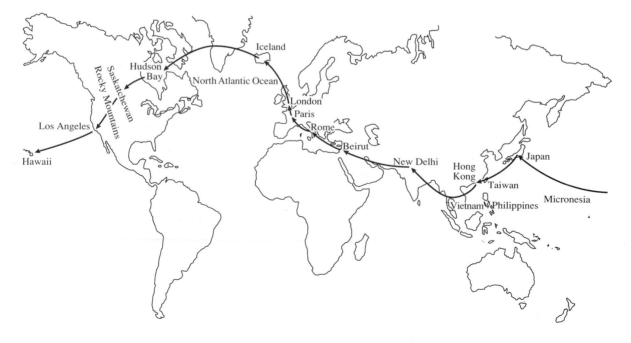

EXERCISE 7-C   *Write articles (a, an, or the) in the blanks when needed. If no article is necessary, write the symbol ∅.*

A QUICK TRIP AROUND THE WORLD—PART II

¹On _____ way to _____ London one has no time to see _____ Changing of _____ Guard, _____ numerous stage productions, _____ Tower of London, or _____ Crown Jewels as _____ plane is soon on its way back to _____ California. ²If it is _____ clear day, one can see icebergs in _____ North Atlantic Ocean. ³_____ short refueling stop in _____ Iceland is _____ only delay on this leg of _____ journey. ⁴One of _____ daylight flights offers _____ spectacular view of _____ Arctic wastes before crossing _____ Hudson Bay and _____ Canada. ⁵Possibly, heavy clouds may block your view of _____ Rocky Mountains and _____ wheat fields of _____ Saskatchewan, but cramped muscles will welcome _____ soon-to-come end of _____ trip. ⁶_____ weary traveler will probably sleep away _____ twenty-four hours he gained by flying _____ west continually. ⁷Possibly _____ prestige value of being able to say one has been around _____ world is _____ only compensation for _____ cost in _____ time, _____ money, and _____ fatigue to make _____ trip. ⁸One could see much more of _____ world in _____ two-hour travelogue movie.

8. Proofreading

As explained previously, an important part of the process of writing is proofreading. Although you now have a better understanding of English nouns and articles, you may still make occasional mistakes with them.

The following exercises will give you practice in focused proofreading. The passages contain numerous mistakes with nouns and articles, but that is the only type of error they contain. Using what you have learned in this chapter, focus on finding and fixing the incorrect nouns and articles.

EXERCISE 8-A   *In the paragraphs below, there are a number of errors involving articles (used unnecessarily, omitted, or incorrectly chosen). Find the errors, correct them, and then rewrite the passage. Do not add, remove, or change any words except articles (a, an, and the).*

CULTURAL DIFFERENCES AND INTERNATIONAL TRADE—PART I

¹Many the people involved in the international trade fail to understand the importance of a cultural differences. ²They do not realize how these differences can directly or indirectly affect the trade. ³Following points demonstrate why it is extremely important for the trading partners to be aware of the foreign customs and a cultural differences.

⁴Germans do not appreciate the premature familiarity. ⁵Therefore, when conducting the business in Germany, an excessive familiarity should be avoided. ⁶For the example, it is considered poor manners to use the first names, except in a long-established relationship. ⁷Instead, the titles, such as Ms. and Mr., are preferable in Germany, as they are in most of the Europe.

EXERCISE 8-B

In the paragraphs below, there are a number of errors involving articles (used unnecessarily, omitted, or incorrectly chosen). Find the errors, correct them, and then rewrite the passage. Do not add, remove, or change any words except articles (a, an, and the).

CULTURAL DIFFERENCES AND INTERNATIONAL TRADE—PART II

[1]Italians, generally speaking, are also different from the Americans, but in a different ways. [2]In the Italy, it is appropriate to give the small business gifts to any subordinate who has helped you during a your visit. [3]Most of the these gifts would not be expected in United States. [4]On other hand, some common U.S. practices, such as asking a person what he or she does for the living, are considered to be in a poor taste in Italy.

[5]In many Arab countries, it is considered impolite to make any the inquiries about female members of a businessman's a family. [6]In the other words, don't ask the business associate, "How is your the wife?" [7]In addition, in Arab nations, having an outer waiting room in office is considered impolite. [8]Therefore, a business interview or the conversation may be held in an office with many the other people who are waiting for their turn. [9]Some of them may even join in your a conversation without being invited. [10]This would be considered extremely rude in United States, but not in Saudi Arabia or the Egypt.

EXERCISE 8-C

In the paragraphs below, there are a number of errors involving articles (used unnecessarily, omitted, or incorrectly chosen). Find the errors, correct them, and then rewrite the passage. Do not add, remove, or change any words except articles (a, an, and the).

CULTURAL DIFFERENCES AND INTERNATIONAL TRADE—PART III

[1]To Chinese people, colors may indicate different ideas than they do to the Americans. [2]For the example, for packaging the product, the red, the gold, and the green are favored, while the color blue is seldom used. [3]Nevertheless, a green hats are to be avoided. [4]Wearing the green hat means that wearer's wife has been unfaithful. [5]Likewise, color white has the special meaning. [6]It is often associated with the funerals.

[7]In the Brazil, the purple is death color and should be avoided. [8]Also, remember the Brazil is an only country in the South America where the official language is the Portuguese. [9]The Brazilians are proud of this the difference and do not appreciate the sales literature in the Spanish.

[10]Businesspeople who are not aware of these differences may commit some serious cross-cultural blunders. [11]Others may be offended when no the offense was actually intended. [12]These misunderstandings may lead to the poor relationships and the lost business opportunities. [13]It certainly pays to be aware.

3

Pronouns and Antecedents

This chapter will help you avoid or correct mistakes like these:

- Electricity is important in our modern world. We use <u>them</u> in our homes, schools, and offices.
- (The first sentence in a composition.) <u>She</u> was born in Chihuahua.
- She rides horses at <u>hers</u> brother's ranch.
- It is a tradition for a Tongan to wear a *ta'ovala* around <u>their</u> waist.
- I don't want that meat or those potatoes because <u>it</u> isn't well done.
- She has a boyfriend, but she doesn't see <u>he</u> very much.
- We saw the dog chasing the cat. Then, a little while later, we saw <u>it</u> stuck in a tree. (Which animal was stuck, the dog or the cat?)
- Mr. and Mrs. Jones are watching the Smith's children at <u>their</u> house. (Whose house are they at, the Jones' or the Smith's?)
- I rushed to the bicycle rack to get my bicycle. I opened the combination lock quickly, sat on <u>it</u>, and started pedaling.
- This problem affects <u>we</u> all.

1. Purpose of Pronouns

Pronouns, though function words, represent nouns (which are content words) or noun phrases. (A chart of English pronouns is found on page 40.) Pronouns are used to avoid unnecessary repetition of the nouns they represent and to allow variety and brevity in writing.

Read the following paragraphs aloud and note how the use of pronouns improves the second paragraph by reducing repetition.

ROCK FESTIVALS

Rock festivals have been extremely popular during the past several years. Rock festivals often last as long as three days. Rock festivals are advertised widely. Rock festivals draw tremendous crowds. Rock festivals attract people from many miles away. Rock festivals feature various popular electronic bands. The various popular electronic bands play for hours on end. The various popular electronic bands play extremely loud music. The extremely loud music doesn't seem to bother the people who attend the rock festivals. The people who attend the rock festivals sometimes listen intently to the rock music and the soloists, but other times the people who attend the rock festivals pay no attention to the rock music or the soloists. The people who attend the rock festivals must enjoy the rock festivals, because the people who attend the rock festivals usually show up at the next rock festival.

ROCK FESTIVALS

Rock festivals have been extremely popular during the past several years. *They* often last as long as three days. *They* are advertised widely, *they* draw tremendous crowds, and *they* attract people from many miles away. Rock festivals feature various popular electronic bands. *They* play for hours on end. *They* play extremely loud music. *This* doesn't seem to bother the people who attend *them*. *They* sometimes listen intently to the rock music and the soloists, but other times *they* pay no attention to *them*. People who attend the rock festivals must enjoy *them*, because *they* usually show up at the next *one*.

EXERCISE 1-A   *In the following story, find the pronouns and underline each of them. Then draw an arrow from each pronoun to its antecedent, and circle the antecedent. (The first one has been done for you.)*

DAVY CROCKETT—PART I

[1]There are many famous (Americans.) [2]Davy Crockett is one of them. [3]He was a famous frontiersman and had a hard but interesting life. [4]This essay will highlight some of the important events in it.

[5]David Crockett was born in the backwoods of Tennessee in 1786. [6]He received only four days of formal schooling. [7]At the age of thirteen, he ran away from home. [8]He didn't return until several years later.

[9]Davy fell in love when he was eighteen, but the girl he loved wanted him to go back to school. [10]To please her, he returned to school for six months, but he didn't enjoy it. [11]In spite of his efforts, she didn't marry him after all, but married someone else.

[12]Davy then left school for good, and he never returned to the classroom. [13]Nevertheless, his lifetime of experiences educated him well.

EXERCISE 1-B   *In the following story, find the pronouns and underline each of them. Then draw an arrow from each pronoun to its antecedent, and circle the antecedent. (The first one has been done for you.)*

DAVY CROCKETT—PART II

[1](Davy Crockett) later married another girl. [2]To start their life together, he and his wife borrowed fifteen dollars. [3]They settled down on a farm, but Davy wasn't

a very good farmer. [4]He was much better at hunting bears. [5]In fact, he shot 105 of them in one year.

[6]Davy was also famous for the tales he told. [7]The people loved to hear him tell them. [8]They also noticed that he was honest and hardworking. [9]Because he understood their frontier life and its challenges, they elected him to the U.S. Congress. [10]He served three terms. [11]People in Washington, D.C. could easily recognize him. [12]He often wore his frontiersman's clothes in that city. [13]His frontier wisdom also attracted a lot of attention. [14]It was refreshing to them.

EXERCISE 1-C *In the following story, find the pronouns and underline each of them. Then draw an arrow from each pronoun to its antecedent, and circle the antecedent. (The first one has been done for you.)*

DAVY CROCKETT—PART III

[1]Davy Crockett was also a soldier. [2]He fought under Andrew Jackson in 1813. [3]Later, Davy went to Texas. [4]He fought in the Battle of the Alamo. [5]The Alamo was a mission turned into a fort. [6]Fewer than two hundred Americans defended it. [7]More than five thousand Mexican soliders attacked it, but they stormed the fort with difficulty. [8]Crockett and the other defenders of the Alamo fought valiantly. [9]They were all killed in the fight.

[10]Davy Crockett has been dead for over a century, but he still lives on in the memories and hearts of the American people. [11]He deserves to be remembered by them. [12]Demonstrating American ideals, he loved freedom above everything else.

2. Pronoun Agreement with Antecedents

2.1 A pronoun must agree in number (singular or plural) and gender (masculine, feminine, or neuter) with its antecedent (the word or words that the pronoun represents).

The boy (singular, masculine) is reading.	He is reading.
The boys (plural, masculine) are reading.	They are reading.
The girl (singular, feminine) is reading.	She is reading.
The girls (plural, feminine) are reading.	They are reading.
The book (singular, neuter) is interesting.	It is interesting.
The books (plural, neuter) are interesting.	They are interesting.

Note: Some antecedents that are normally neuter may be personified (treated as if they were human beings) and take masculine or feminine pronouns.

Mr. Winter brings cold wind and lots of snow. When **he** arrives, I want to leave.

The ship was hit by two enemy torpedoes, and **she** sank.

San Francisco is my hometown, and I think **she's** the most beautiful city in the world.

Davy Crockett's favorite rifle was called "Betsy," and he always took good care of **her**.

Pronoun Chart—Personal Pronouns

	Subjective		Objective		Possessive				Reflexive	
					MODIFIER		*PRONOUN*			
	Singular	*Plural*	*Singular*	*Plural*	*Singular*	*Plural*	*Singular*	*Plural*	*Singular*	*Plural*
1st Person	I	we	me	us	my	our	mine	ours	myself	ourselves
2nd Person	you	you	you	you	your	your	yours	yours	yourself	yourselves
3rd Person										
masculine	he	they	him	them	his	their	his	theirs	himself	themselves
feminine	she	they	her	them	her	their	hers	theirs	herself	themselves
neuter	it	they	it	them	its	their	its	theirs	itself	themselves

Demonstratives

that	those
this	these

Note: Interrogative pronouns (*who, whom, whose, which, what, where, when, why, how*) are discussed in Chapter 7, section 11.
Relative pronouns (*who, whom, whose, which, that*) are discussed in Chapter 12, section 2.

2.2 Pronouns representing the same antecedent have **subjective, objective, possessive,** and **reflexive** forms. **Subjective** pronouns are used in subject position.

> **Mary** is competent. **She** is also efficient.

Objective pronouns are used in object positions.

> The personnel manager hired **Mary.**
> Mary's co-workers like **her.** (object of verb)
> The supervisor is happy with **her.** (object of preposition)

Possessive pronouns are used in place of possessives (noun + *'s*).

> Mary's work is challenging. **Her** hours are long.

Reflexive pronouns are used:

1. as objects when the subject and the object are the same thing.

> Mary forces **herself** to get the job done.

2. for emphasis.

> She **herself** sets the pace.

2.3 In writing, *I* always represents the **writer**, and *you* the *reader*. For this reason it is not usually necessary to use or state the antecedent for these pronouns.

In formal writing, *one* is often used instead of *you* when an impersonal pronoun is desired (the possessive form of *one* is *one's* or *his*).

> **You** should hand in **your** homework on time.
> **One** should hand in **his** homework on time. (formal)
> **One** should hand in **one's** homework on time. (more formal)

EXERCISE 2-A *In the following passage, substitute the correct pronoun for each of the italicized nouns.*

TOKYO

[1]Tokyo is the largest city in the world. [2]*Tokyo's* population is over twenty-five million. [3]It is predicted that by the year 2000 *Tokyo's population* will be nearly thirty million.

[4]Tokyo is also the capital of Japan. [5]Since 1603, *Tokyo* has been the political, economic, and cultural center of Japan. [6]In that year, Tokugawa Ieyasu (a man) set up *Tokugawa Ieyasu's* shogunate in a castle town. [7]*The castle town* was then called Edo. [8]During the Meiji Restoration in 1868, *Edo's* name was changed to Tokyo.

[9]Tokyo has been destroyed many times, by fire, earthquake, and bombing. [10]The people of Tokyo have never abandoned *the people of Tokyo's* city. [11]*The people of Tokyo*

have rebuilt *Tokyo* every time *Tokyo* has been destroyed. [12]Each time, Tokyo has recovered from destruction to become an even greater city than before.

EXERCISE 2-B   *In the following passage, substitute the correct pronoun for each of the italicized nouns.*

MOUNT FUJI

[1]Mount Fuji is Japan's most famous mountain. [2]*Mount Fuji* is also Japan's highest mountain. [3]*Mount Fuji* rises 3,776 meters above sea level. [4]Mount Fuji is unique because of *Mount Fuji's* cone shape and the way *Mount Fuji* rises from the surrounding plain.

[5]There are three mountain-climbing paths on Mount Fuji. [6]Buses that travel on the mountain highways carry passengers up to the 1,500-meter level. [7]Many people ride on *the buses that travel on the mountain highways*. [8]Some of the people then try to climb to the top of Mount Fuji. [9]These people are Japanese as well as foreign tourists. [10]All of *these people* do not make it to the top. [11]Climbing Mount Fuji is not easy. [12]*Climbing Mount Fuji* can be very difficult for the unprepared climber.

[13]Many visitors to Mount Fuji do not try to climb *Mount Fuji*. [14]*Many visitors to Mount Fuji* are content to view Mount Fuji from a distance. [15]*Many visitors to Mount Fuji* prefer to spend *many visitors to Mount Fuji's* time seeing the many other beautiful sights of Japan.

EXERCISE 2-C   *In the following passage, substitute the correct pronoun for each of the italicized nouns.*

HOKKAIDO

[1]Hokkaido is the northernmost island of Japan. [2]*Hokkaido* has not been developed very much because of *Hokkaido's* distance from the main island of Honshu.

[3]Hokkaido's climate is quite cold. [4]*Hokkaido's* average year-round temperature is five to seven degrees Centigrade. [5]In January, the temperature may drop to ten degrees Centigrade below zero.

[6]Sapporo is the political, economic, and cultural center of Hokkaido. [7]*Sapporo* was the site of the 1972 Winter Olympics. [8]Athletes from all over the world traveled to Sapporo. [9]*The athletes from all over the world* competed in skiing, ice skating, and other winter sports. [10]Tourists from all over the world came to watch *the athletes from all over the world* compete.

[11]Hokkaido's annual attraction is the Snow Festival. [12]*The Snow Festival* is held in Sapporo every February. [13]Sapporo's central plaza is filled with gigantic sculptures of historical, modern, and imaginary characters made of snow. [14]*The gigantic sculptures of historical, modern, and imaginary characters made of snow* are very impressive. [15]*The gigantic sculptures of historical, modern, and imaginary characters made of snow* may be over twenty feet high. [16]*The gigantic sculptures of historical, modern, and imaginary characters made of snow* look like dragons, samurai warriors, or even famous Japanese temples. [17]Visitors from far away travel to Sapporo to look at *the gigantic sculptures of historical, modern, and imaginary characters made of snow*.

3. Clarity of Pronoun Antecedents

The antecedent of a pronoun must be clear to the reader. In a paragraph, the noun (antecedent) is usually stated near the beginning. Pronouns may then be used in place of the same noun later, unless (1) other possible antecedents have the same number (singular or plural) and gender (masculine, feminine, or neuter), and/or (2) pronouns are used excessively.

If the use of a pronoun may be confusing to the reader, use the full noun or noun phrase instead of the pronoun. Here is an example of confusing pronoun use:

EXAMPLE PARAGRAPH
Trees are useful to man. The leaves give off oxygen. The trunks and branches provide wood. I feel sad when they fall to the ground.

Which of these drawings is described in the example paragraph?

The example paragraph is confusing because the pronoun *they* could refer to *leaves, trees,* or *branches.*

The occasional use of the antecedent noun can improve a composition, particularly when the topic emphasis changes. Compare the use of nouns and pronouns in these two paragraphs.

COCONUT TREES

Coconut trees grow in tropical and semi-tropical climates. *They* grow almost anywhere. *They* grow on the seashore, and *they* grow at higher elevations. *They* are very useful, as *they* provide most of man's necessities. *They* provide food for people, and *they* furnish fuel for fires. *They* provide oil for soap and other products. *They* supply material for building houses. *They* furnish shade either as trees or when woven as blinds, and *they* are used for mats and clothing.

COCONUT TREES

Coconut trees grow in tropical and semi-tropical climates. *They* grow almost anywhere. *They* grow on the seashore, and *they* grow at higher elevations. *Coconut trees* are very useful, as *they* provide most of man's necessities. *They* provide food for people and *they* furnish fuel for fires. *They* provide oil for soap and other products. *They* supply material for building houses. *Coconut trees* furnish shade either as trees or when woven as blinds, and *they* are used for mats and clothing.

EXERCISE 3-A   *In the following passage, substitute pronouns for nouns where appropriate. You must decide which nouns should be replaced by pronouns and which pronouns should be used to replace them. Make sure that each pronoun you use clearly refers to its antecedent and agrees with it.*

OCEANS

[1]The earth is a water world. [2]Oceans dominate the earth. [3]Oceans cover over two-thirds of the earth. [4]Oceans regulate the weather. [5]So far, man has utilized only the available arable land. [6]Man is rapidly exhausting the available arable land's resources. [7]The ocean may be the answer to man's needs. [8]Up until now, the ocean has been used only as a highway for ships and as a hunting ground for fishermen. [9]The ocean may provide man with food and minerals. [10]The ocean has more plants and animals than the land. [11]Ocean currents have been charted, but man must know much more about the ocean if man is to use the ocean for man's

advantage. [12]Can man use the ocean as a dumping ground for man's radioactive waste and then expect to eat the ocean's produce? [13]If man contaminates the ocean, can man still expect the ocean to retain the ocean's productivity?

EXERCISE 3-B   *In the following passage, substitute pronouns for nouns where appropriate. You must decide which nouns should be replaced by pronouns and which pronouns should be used to replace them. Make sure that each pronoun you use clearly refers to its antecedent and agrees with it.*

TYPEWRITERS

[1]Until 1867 people had to write in longhand. [2]Although people could use feather quills, steel pen points, fountain pens, and pencils, people still had to write in longhand.

[3]Typewriters are mechanical instruments that make an impression on paper when keys are struck. [4]Typewriters are used in homes, schools, offices, etc. [5]Almost all secretaries use typewriters daily.

[6]The typewriter was invented in 1867 by a United States journalist. [7]The typewriter was patented by a United States journalist in 1868.

[8]Manual typewriters were used for many years. [9]Manual typewriters can be used anywhere. [10]Manual typewriters do not use electricity. [11]The highest recorded speeds for typing on a manual typewriter are listed in the *Guinness Book of World Records*. [12]The highest speeds for typing on a manual typewriter are 170 words per minute for one minute and an average of 147 words per minute for one hour of steady typing.

[13]Electric typewriters are now used in many places. [14]Electric typewriters are easier to use and typists can attain higher speeds on electric typewriters. [15]The official record on an electric typewriter is 216 words per minute. [16]For one hour, the official record on an electric typewriter is 149 words per minute.

EXERCISE 3-C   *In the following passage, substitute pronouns for nouns where appropriate. You must decide which nouns should be replaced by pronouns and which pronouns should be used to replace them. Make sure each pronoun you use clearly refers to its antecedent and agrees with it.*

CONSTANTINE

[1]The first Christian ruler of the Roman Empire was Constantine I. [2]The first Christian ruler of the Roman Empire was also known as Constantine the Great. [3]The first Christian ruler of the Roman Empire's full name was Flavius Valerius Aurelius Constantinus. [4]The first Christian ruler of the Roman Empire was born about 280 A.D..

[5]Constantine fought as a soldier in Egypt and Persia. [6]Constantine's father was also a soldier and one of the rulers of the Roman Empire. [7]Constantine and Constantine's father fought together in Britain.

[8]Constantine became a Christian in an unusual way. [9]In the year 312 A.D. Constantine marched on Rome with Constantine's armies to attack Maxentius, his rival. [10]The night before the battle, Constantine had a vision. [11]The vision convinced Constantine to become a Christian. [12]Constantine saw a flaming cross in the sky. [13]Beneath the flaming cross in the sky the words "By this sign thou shalt conquer" were written. [14]Constantine adopted the cross as a symbol. [15]Constantine had the cross put on the sails of Constantine's ships. [16]Constantine's men put the cross on Constantine's men's shields and flags. [17]The next day, Constantine defeated Maxentius.

[18]After defeating all of Constantine's other rivals, Constantine became the only ruler of the entire Roman world. [19]Sunday became the day of worship. [20]Later,

Constantine ordered a meeting held at Nicaea. [21]The meeting's purpose was to settle disputes over Christ's divinity.

[22]In the year 330 A.D., Constantine established a new capital in the East. [23]The new capital in the East was named Constantinople—"The City of Constantine." [24]Today, "The City of Constantine" is called Istanbul.

4. Dummy Subjects

A "dummy subject" is used because in written English every sentence must have a subject, but in some cases the true subject is unknown or nonexistent. In such cases, a dummy subject may be used. It stands in the sentence position where the true subject normally does, in much the same way "dummies" (mannequins) take the place of real people in store window displays.

4.1 When *it* is used as a dummy subject, it does not have an antecedent. It is not possible to draw an arrow from the *it* to a preceding noun which it refers to (as you did in exercises 1-A, B, C).

> It rains a lot here.
> It's a warm day.

In some cases the true subject can be shifted toward the end of the sentence. (This process is explained in Chapter 13, section 6.) The dummy subject *it* then takes the original subject's place.

> It is hard to believe what you say. (To believe what you say is hard.)
> It's a miracle that he survived. (That he survived is a miracle.)

4.2 *There* is also a dummy subject. It is used with a form of *be* (*is, are, was*, etc.) or a verb like *seem* or *appear* to express the idea that something exists. In this case, aux-word or verb agreement depends on the noun or noun phrase that follows the verb or aux-word rather than on the dummy subject *there*.

> There **is** an apple in the basket. (singular count noun)
> There **are** several apples in the basket. (plural count noun)
> There **is** excitement in the air. (noncount noun)
> There **seems** to be some trouble here. (noun phrase)

Note that *there*, like the dummy subject *it*, has no meaning in and of itself. It only functions as a dummy subject, permitting the true subject noun or noun phrase to follow.

There is also an adverb of place that designates a certain location already mentioned or a location not near the speaker. One test to determine whether *there* is functioning as a dummy subject or an adverb in a particular sentence is to change the sentence into a question using *where*. If the word *there* answers that question, it is an adverb. If it does not answer the *where* question but indicates that something exists, *there* is a dummy subject.

EXERCISE 4-A

In the following paragraph, each it *has been italicized and numbered. Label each* it *with a* P *if it is a pronoun and a* D *if it is a dummy subject. For each pronoun, draw an arrow to its antecedent.*

A COLD DAY

It's now the middle of winter and *it's* a very cold day. The temperature
 1   2

outside is fifteen degrees Fahrenheit, and *it* is dropping steadily. *It* has been a
                                           3   4

long time since anyone has felt comfortable outside. Inside the house *it* is warm
                                                                      5

and cozy. I have a fire and *it* keeps me warm. *It* is pleasant to watch the flame
                            6   7

flicker as *it* throws shadows on the walls. However, *it* is necessary for me to go
           8   9

outside and bring in some more wood if I expect to keep *it* burning during the
                                                        10

night. *It* is a task I dread, but the sooner I do *it* the sooner I can return to my
       11   12

pleasant room and *its* cozy comfort. I had better get at *it.*
                   13   14

EXERCISE 4-B

In the following paragraphs, each it *has been italicized and numbered. Label each* it *with a* P *if it is a pronoun and a* D *if it is a dummy subject. For each pronoun, draw an arrow to its antecedent.*

A GARDEN

It is spring. Suddenly, *it's* time to get out-of-doors and get to work. *It* rains
 1   2   3

a lot during the spring, so *it's* necessary to work when one can. *It* is necessary
                            4   5

to trim the deadwood from the trees and shrubs. *It's* important to oil the lawn
                                                6

mower as *it* may have rusted a bit during the winter. The garden must be
         7

planted. *It* should have vegetables as well as flowers.
         8

When summer comes, *it* would be nice to go fishing, but the garden needs a
                    9

lot of care. *It* needs to be cultivated. *It* also needs to be watered and weeded. *It*
             10   11   12

seems that the work never ends.

It pays dividends, however, to raise a garden. In addition to the satisfaction of
13

seeing things grow, *it* produces food for the body and flowers for the soul.
                    14

EXERCISE 4-C   *In the following paragraph, each* it *has been italicized and numbered. Label each* it *with a P if it is a pronoun and a D if it is a dummy subject. For each pronoun, draw an arrow to its antecedent.*

DAYDREAMS

Most of us, like Walter Mitty,* have performed a heroic deed or two. *It*
1
might have been one of courage, *it* might have been one of strength, or *it*
2   3
might have been one of nobility. *It* is amazing what one can accomplish when
4
he daydreams. *It* seems like nothing is impossible. *It* may be dangerous to
5   6
daydream, since *it* is a jolt when the dream is over and reality calls one back
7
to the real world. *It* may be very hard to achieve the dream, so one might not
8
even attempt *it* even though *it* is possible. On the other hand, when the dream
9   10
is impossible to achieve in reality, *it* is better not to attempt to achieve *it*. *It* is
11   12 13
fun to dream, though, isn't *it*?
14

*James Thurber, "The Secret Life of Walter Mitty," *My World and Welcome to It* (New York: Harcourt Brace Jovanovich, 1937).

EXERCISE 4.1-A   *In the following paragraph, each* there *has been italicized and numbered. Label each* there *with a D if it is a dummy subject and a P if it indicates a place.*

FAIRY TALES

There are many fairy tales in story books. Found *there* are "Jack and
1   2
the Beanstalk" and "Cinderella." *There* is also an old favorite of mine—
3
"Rumpelstiltskin." "Beauty and the Beast" is *there* too. *There* seems to be a
4   5
strange fascination in these often-told tales for young and old. In my mind's eye
I can still see the books *there* on the shelf in my old room. *There* is my mother,
6   7
too, and the rocking chair she sat in as she read these stories to me. *There* were
8
books of nursery rhymes *there* too, along with the fairy tales. *There* were "Little
9   10
Boy Blue," "Goosey, Goosey Gander," and "Little Jack Horner" within those
pages. Today *there* are cartoons and TV programs to take the place of the fairy
11
tales. *There* seems to be too much competition for the princes and princesses,
12
the ogres and the witches that are found *there* in the old silent books.
13

EXERCISE 4.1-B   *In the following paragraphs, each* there *has been italicized and numbered. Label each* there *with a* D *if it is a dummy subject and a* P *if it indicates a place.*

THE CIRCUS

Everyone who is young at heart loves a circus. *There* are acts involving
₁

clowns, trapeze artists, high wire performers, and trained animals. Wild animals

are *there* as well. *There* are also side shows to view the fat man, the bearded
₂   ₃

lady, and other sights, so be sure to take some extra money when you go *there.*
₄

There may also be guessing games and games of chance in addition to a
₅

huge Ferris wheel and other enticing rides. It's fun for the family to go *there,*
₆

as *there* is sure to be something for everybody—young and old. *There* are so
₇   ₈

many things to see and hear at a three-ring circus that it is impossible to take

in everything. Hopefully, they'll all be *there* again when the circus rolls around
₉

next time, so save your money and we'll plan on going again next year.

EXERCISE 4.1-C   *In the following paragraph, each* there *has been italicized and numbered. Label each* there *with a* D *if it is a dummy subject and a* P *if it indicates a place.*

THE ICEMAN

In grandmother's day *there* were many occupations that do not exist today.
₁

For example, *there* was the iceman. He had a large truck with a big insulated
₂

box on the back. Huge blocks of ice were kept *there.* He delivered sections of
₃

these to houses along his route. He would look at the windows and, if cards

were displayed *there,* he would chip off the amount of ice indicated on the card.
₄

Then, the iceman would seize the piece with his tongs, sling it over his leather-

clad shoulder, carry it into the house, and once *there* place it in the ice box. The
₅

woman of the house often had to mop up the watery trail left by the melting

ice. *There* were always lots of children in the street around the van waiting
₆

to catch any small chips of ice that might fall *there.* Occasionally, *there* was a
₇   ₈

friendly iceman who would chip off a few small fragments and toss them into

the crowd of children who vied with one another to be the lucky recipient of

a cold chunk of ice. Automatic refrigeration has brought an end to the coming

of the iceman, but *there* are many who still recall those good old days with
₉

nostalgia.

EXERCISE 4.2-A   *In the following passage, there are many dummy subjects. Write either* is *or* are *in the blank provided after (or before) the dummy subject.*

TONIGHT'S NEWSPAPER

"_____ there anything interesting in the newspaper tonight?"
1

"Well, there _____ an interesting story about the president's new budget
2

plan. There _____ some news about that big hurricane in the Gulf of Mexico.
3

And there _____ the usual comics."
4

"No, no. I mean really interesting."

"Well, there _____ some interesting letters and responses in Dear Gabby's
5

advice column. There _____ a good story about how to save energy in your
6

home. And there _____ a critical editorial about government waste."
7

"I guess you don't understand. I want to know if there _____ anything
8

about last night's football game."

EXERCISE 4.2-B   *In the following passage, there are many dummy subjects. Write either* was *or* were *in the blank provided after (or before) the dummy subject.*

THE CIRCUS

Last night we went to the circus. It was really good. There _____ acrobats
1

swinging on the trapeze, and there _____ one who did a triple somersault.
2

There _____ an act with trained lions and tigers. When the trainer gave the
3

command, they jumped through a flaming hoop. There _____ also dozens
4

of funny clowns. In one act, they drove out in a small car and got out one by

one. I couldn't believe it, but there _____ ten clowns and a small dog in that
5

tiny car! Of course, there _____ also vendors selling hot peanuts and popcorn
6

and cold drinks. It's funny, though; there _____ no candy for sale. At least,
7

I didn't see any. Maybe they ran out. That's all right. There _____ plenty of
8

other things to make me happy at the circus last night.

EXERCISE 4.2-C   *In the following passage, there are many dummy subjects. Write either* is *or* are *in the blank provided after (or before) the dummy subject.*

PERSONAL MANAGEMENT

There _____ many devices on the market to help you organize and manage
1

your life. There _____ daily, weekly, and monthly planning calendars. There
2

_____ prepared pads of "to do" lists. There _____ time-management
seminars, and there _____ a lot of books that will teach you principles and
procedures for managing your time effectively. And there _____ more than
one device which combines a calendar, "to do" list, and guidance all in one
package. For me, however, there _____ one device that works best. I simply
tie a string around my finger. It reminds me that there _____ something
important that I need to do. Of course, sometimes there _____ several strings
on my fingers and I get confused and people stare at my hands, but this simple
method usually works fine for me.

5. Proofreading

As explained previously, an important part of the process of writing is proofreading.
Although you now have a better understanding of English pronouns and how they
are used, you may still make occasional mistakes with them.

The following exercises will give you practice in focused proofreading. The passages contain numerous mistakes with pronouns, but that is the only type of error
they contain. Using what you have learned in this chapter, focus on finding and
fixing the incorrect pronouns.

EXERCISE 5-A   _In the paragraphs below, there are a number of errors involving pronouns (wrong
form, lack of agreement with antecedent, unclear antecedent. etc.) and dummy subjects.
Find the errors, correct them, and then rewrite the passage. Do not add, remove, or
change any words except pronouns and dummy subjects (and their accompanying verbs
and_ be _aux-words)._

MULTINATIONAL CORPORATIONS

[1]Multinational corporations are corporations that operate in several different
countries at the same time and have at least twenty percent of its total sales,
assets, or labor force in foreign subsidiaries. [2]It must have both production and
marketing strategies relevant to a world market. [3]Today there is thousands of these
corporations.

[4]Typically, multinational corporations use their funds to buy or build plants
and other facilities in foreign countries. [5]Many of they began as single-nation
companies with large amounts of exports. [6]With the passage of time, however, it
found itself hampered by trade restrictions, foreign exchange difficulties, and high
transportation costs. [7]Faced with this problem, they decided to put down roots in
selected foreign ("host") countries. [8]Themselves have a local management staff,
which is supervised by parent-company officials back in the original country.

[9]Of course, no two multinational corporations are exactly alike. [10]Each one
has theirs distinctive characteristics. [11]They all differ in size, purpose, investment
strategy, localities, operating philosophy, and many other variables.

EXERCISE 5-B

In the paragraphs below, there are a number of errors involving pronouns (wrong form, lack of agreement with antecedent, unclear antecedent, etc.) and dummy subjects. Find the errors, correct them, and then rewrite the passage. Do not add, remove, or change any words except pronouns and dummy subjects (and their accompanying verbs and be aux-words).

DEDICATED FOOTBALL FANS

[1]Many sports fans are dedicated to a particular team. [2]He knows their members' names and his numbers. [3]They always cheer for they team and watch as many games as he can—either on television or in person. [4]There is many such fans. [5]In fact, your probably know one yourself.

[6]One particular fan, however, stands out for their dedication. [7]Miles Pellerin has attended seven hundred consecutive University of Southern California football games. [8]Now 83 years old, Pellerin attended he first USC football game in 1927 when he was a student at Southern Cal. [9]They graduated in 1929, but they didn't stop going to football games. [10]In fact, over the years, he has attended every USC football game in person, whether itself was at home or away. [11]In doing so, his has traveled to about fifty cities in thirty-five different states.

[12]Pellerin's streak just about came to an end in 1949 when there was in the hospital because of a ruptured appendix. [13]His entered the hospital and had his operation on Tuesday. [14]Later in the week, when he asked the doctor if he could go to the game on Saturday, he said, "No chance!" [15]But on Saturday he was at the game. [16]His got up, told the nurse himself was going for a walk, and then called him brother. [17]A few minutes later, he brother picked him up in its car and took themselves to the game. [18]Now, that's real dedication!

EXERCISE 5-C

In the paragraphs below, there are a number of errors involving pronouns (wrong form, lack of agreement with antecedent, unclear antecedent, etc.) and dummy subjects. Find the errors, correct them, and then rewrite the passage. Do not add, remove, or change any words except pronouns and dummy subjects (and their accompanying verbs and be aux-words).

IS THIS MEETING REALLY NECESSARY?

[1]There are times when you should call a meeting, and times when you shouldn't. [2]Next time your feel like holding a meeting, he should ask himself, "Is this meeting really necessary?"

[3]There is two main reasons for holding a meeting. [4]One is to share information with those who need to know them. [5]The second is to solve problems.

[6]An information-sharing meeting is worth holding when they have to explain a plan or project. [7]Its is also appropriate when there is a need to report on accomplishments. [8]They are also good when you need to gain support for an idea.

[9]A problem-solving meeting is worthwhile when you need to define or solve a problem. [10]In addition, they are often necessary when your need to get people to agree on a decision. [11]Many problems are like puzzles. [12]It is made of many pieces, and to solve them, you need to bring together (in a meeting) all the people who hold the key pieces.

[13]There is two other reasons for holding meetings. [14]One is to train people how to do something, such as filling out a report form. [15]Another is to build morale or recognize their achievements. [16]Employees usually work for more than just money. [17]Meetings that build participants' sense of mission and/or feeling of commitment or her feelings of self-worth are always worthwhile.

4

Aux-Words

This chapter will help you avoid or correct mistakes like these:

- We've should taken more money.
- She've been teaching for many years.
- They have given you help with your paper?
- Does George works here?
- Dora ___ born in Guatemala.
- It sounds terrible, isn't it?
- Why ___ you think electricity is important?
- Some of them ___ not need a car.

1. Forms of Aux-Words

A very important and powerful kind of function word in modern English is the auxiliary. These words are often called *helping* or *auxiliary verbs* and/or *modals.* Some books call them *operators, green words,* or *x-words.* In this book we call them **aux-words.**

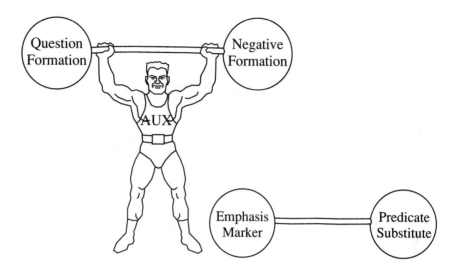

Following are some of the common English aux-words:

> *is, am, are, was, were* (forms of *be*)
> *do, does, did* (forms of *do*)
> *have, has, had* (forms of *have*)
> *can, could, will, would, shall, should, may, might, must* (modals)

Contractions combining aux-words with *not* are also considered aux-words.

> *isn't, aren't, wasn't, weren't*
> *don't, doesn't, didn't*
> *haven't, hasn't, hadn't*
> *can't, couldn't, won't, wouldn't, shouldn't, mustn't*

Some two-word aux-word combinations also exist:

> *ought to, had better, would rather*

They function much the way single-word aux-words do, with a few exceptions (e.g., only the first word is moved when asking questions; the negative marker *not* is often placed between the two words).

EXERCISE 1-A   *Find the aux-words in the passage below. Underline or circle them.*

BLACKBOARDS

¹Blackboards are very useful things. ²Educators, businessmen, or scientists can use them in their work. ³A well-used blackboard can be an invaluable aid to communication.

⁴Many people don't appreciate the advantages of blackboards. ⁵A blackboard doesn't cost a lot of money. ⁶It doesn't require electricity or gasoline. ⁷You can use it over and over. ⁸You can write on it. ⁹You can erase the writing easily. ¹⁰You can then write something else in the same place.

¹¹Blackboard use is not without its hazards. ¹²Misusing a blackboard will result in problems. ¹³An uncared-for blackboard will deteriorate. ¹⁴The surface will crack. ¹⁵It may get too smooth to use.

¹⁶A teacher may purposely misuse a blackboard to wake up sleeping students. ¹⁷Scratching fingernails on a blackboard will make a terrible noise. ¹⁸Holding a piece of chalk the wrong way will also result in an awful sound. ¹⁹Ignorance may also cause people to mistreat a blackboard. ²⁰Everyone should learn to use a blackboard properly.

EXERCISE 1-B   *Find the aux-words in the passage below. Underline or circle them.*

CRABS

¹Crabs are strange animals. ²These shellfish can live in or out of water. ³Their five pairs of walking legs are long and spindly but strong. ⁴Their muscles are inside their skeleton. ⁵A crab's eyes are found on movable stalks. ⁶They can be extended or retracted. ⁷Crabs don't walk forward. ⁸Crabs don't walk backward. ⁹They can only walk sideways.

¹⁰There are many different kinds of crabs. ¹¹Hermit crabs must live in shells discarded by other sea creatures. ¹²When they outgrow one shell, they must find another, larger one. ¹³The tiny pea crab can be found living inside the shell of an oyster. ¹⁴The giant king crab may measure ten feet from tip to tip of its claws. ¹⁵In spring, tropical land crabs may be seen migrating by the thousands to the sea to lay their eggs. ¹⁶Nothing will stop them or make them change course. ¹⁷The fiddler crab is the type most commonly seen on the beach. ¹⁸Some types of crabs are valued as food. ¹⁹Others are not good to eat. ²⁰All crabs are fascinating to observe.

EXERCISE 1-C   *Find the aux-words in the passage below. Underline or circle them.*

LEARNING A NEW LANGUAGE

¹Learning a new language is usually hard work. ²Students must spend many hours speaking, reading, and writing the new language. ³They are required to do many exercises which may be uninteresting or even boring. ⁴They may also have to spend many hours in a language lab where they must concentrate on the sounds of the new tongue so they will recognize these sounds and also so they can produce them. ⁵The sounds and grammar of a new language are often quite different from those of the student's native tongue and thus may be confusing to the learner. ⁶Many times students feel they have mastered the new language, only to find that they cannot communicate with native speakers. ⁷Many will give up their study while others will renew their efforts to master the new tongue.

2. Subject/Aux-Word Agreement (Present Tense)

In the present tense, some aux-words have more than one form. The correct form to use depends on the subject of the sentence it is used in.

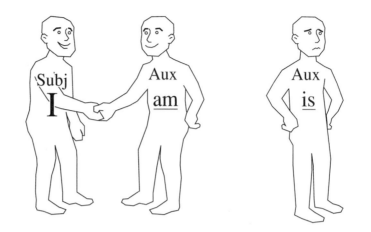

Use...	when the subject is...	Example Sentences
am	the pronoun *I*	I *am* studying English.
is	a singular noun a singular pronoun (except *you*) a noncount noun an *-ing* noun phrase (see Chapter 13)	The boy *is* studying English. He *is* studying French also. Mathematics *is* important. Studying diligently *is* a challenge.
are	a plural noun a plural pronoun the pronoun *you* (singular or plural)	The boys *are* studying English. They *are* studying French also. You *are* studying English.
has	a singular noun a singular pronoun (except *you*) a noncount noun an *-ing* noun phrase (see Chapter 13)	The boy *has* studied English for a long time. He *has* studied French a long time also. His dedication *has* been admirable. Studying languages *has* been rewarding.
have	the pronoun *I* the pronoun *you* (singular or plural) a plural noun a plural pronoun	I *have* studied English for a long time. You *have* studied English a long time. The boys *have* studied English a long time. They *have* studied French a long time also.
does	a singular noun a singular pronoun (except *you*) a noncount noun an *-ing* noun phrase (see Chapter 13)	The boy *does* not write welll. He *does* not read well either. Failure *does* not usually require effort. Learning to write *does* require effort.
do	the pronoun *I* the pronoun *you* (singular or plural) a plural noun a plural pronoun	I *do* not write well. You *do* not write well. The boys *do* not write well. They *do* not read well either.

Modal aux-words have only one form. This same form is used regardless of whether the subject is singular, plural, noncount, etc. For example:

Use...	when the subject is...	Example Sentences
will	a singular noun a plural noun a noncount noun a singular pronoun (except *you*) a plural pronoun the pronoun *I* the pronoun *you* (singular or plural) an *-ing* noun phrase (see Chapter 13)	The boy *will* write well. The boys *will* also write well. Success *will* require effort. He *will* read well also. They *will* read well also. I *will* write well. You *will* write well. Learning to write *will* require effort.

EXERCISE 2-A   *Write* is *or* are, *whichever is correct, in the blanks.*

CROCODILIANS—PART I

¹The crocodile and alligator _____ reptiles, a major class of animals that also includes snakes, lizards, and turtles. ²There _____ about twenty-five species of reptiles belonging to a group called crocodilians. ³Crocodiles, alligators, caymans, and gavials _____ all crocodilians.

⁴A crocodilian _____ not very pretty. ⁵Small bony plates and scales _____ all over its body. ⁶Its long jaws, sharp teeth, and ugly appearance _____ terrifying to many people.

⁷All crocodilians _____ similar, but there _____ ways of telling one type of crocodilian from another. ⁸The snout of the true crocodile _____ long and tapering. ⁹The head _____ almost triangular. ¹⁰The snout of the alligator _____ broad and rounded. ¹¹The cayman's snout _____ also broad and rounded, but the snout of a gavial _____ extremely long and thin.

¹²Crocodilians _____ capable of making all kinds of noises. ¹³Booming, barking, croaking, and grunting _____ only a few of them.

EXERCISE 2-B   *Write* is *or* are, *whichever is correct, in the blanks.*

CROCODILIANS—PART II

¹All crocodilians _____ excellent swimmers. ²Their long powerful tails _____ good for propelling them through the water. ³Their short legs _____ nearly useless, so they hold them close to the body as they swim.

⁴A crocodilian's body _____ perfect for floating at the water's surface. ⁵Its eyes, ears, and nostrils _____ on the top of its head and snout. ⁶They remain above the waterline while the rest of the crocodilian's body _____ floating beneath the surface.

⁷A crocodilian _____ also capable of diving beneath the surface. ⁸Some crocodilians _____ capable of staying under water for as long as five hours at a time.

⁹Crocodilians _____ good hunters also. ¹⁰Sometimes a crocodilian floats just beneath the surface waiting to snap up a duck, muskrat, or other water animal that _____ swimming by. ¹¹Animals as large as deer and cattle _____ fair game for a large crocodilian. ¹²It grips them with its strong jaws and drags them into the water. ¹³Once the prey _____ in the water, the crocodilian drags it beneath the surface to drown. ¹⁴All crocodilians, even smaller ones, _____ dangerous when cornered or wounded.

EXERCISE 2-C   *Write* is *or* are, *whichever is correct, in the blanks.*

CROCODILIANS—PART III

¹The nests of some crocodilians _____ large heaps of plant materials. ²Others _____ simply holes scooped in a riverbank. ³In a single nest there may be from twenty to ninety crocodilian eggs. ⁴The eggs _____ long and white with a hard, thick shell.

⁵Crocodilians _____ tiny when they _____ born. ⁶Newborn crocodilians _____ easy prey for other animals. ⁷A recently hatched crocodilian _____ almost defenseless. ⁸Larger animals eat many young crocodilians.

⁹Once it reaches adulthood, however, a large crocodilian _____ relatively safe. ¹⁰It _____ possible for it to live a long time. ¹¹The oldest alligators on record _____ more than fifty years old. ¹²Some crocodilians _____ very large when they _____ grown. ¹³For example, an average adult American alligator weighs about 500 pounds.

¹⁴If there _____ a long period of hot, dry weather, the crocodilian buries itself deep in the mud. ¹⁵If the weather _____ too cold, crocodilians go into a deep winter sleep called hibernation. ¹⁶They wake up when conditions _____ better.

EXERCISE 2.1-A   *Write* have *or* has, *whichever is correct, in the blanks.*

A DISCOURAGING DAY

¹_____ life ever disappointed you unexpectedly? ²_____ a day ever discouraged you completely? ³If so, you can sympathize with me. ⁴Today _____ been a very discouraging day for me. ⁵I _____ had a very difficult time. ⁶I _____ tried to do many things, but not a single one _____ succeeded. ⁷I made great plans at the beginning of the day, but now, as I look back, all my plans _____ failed. ⁸So many things _____ backfired today that I don't even dare try anything else. ⁹I feel like going back to bed. ¹⁰Everything _____ gone wrong and I _____ lost hope that anything will turn out right. ¹¹It seems like everything _____ been a

disappointment. [12]I _____ had difficult days before, but there _____ never been one like today. [13]I hope you _____ never had a day like this.

EXERCISE 2.1-B   *Write* have *or* has, *whichever is correct, in the blanks.*

SUCCESS IN LIFE

[1]I _____ always dreamed of being a great success. [2]Although I _____ attempted many things, however, I still _____ not found anything that I _____ been successful at or that _____ appealed to me.

[3]Other members of my family _____ all been successful. [4]My father _____ become a captain in the Air Force. [5]My mother _____ been elected to Congress. [6]Although it _____ taken him seven years, one of my brothers _____ just graduated from college. [7]My sister _____ earned her degree in medicine. [8]My other brother is not the academic type, but he _____ been very successful as an explorer. [9]He _____ just discovered a new tributary to the Amazon River which _____ been named after him.

[10]I'm the only one in the family who _____ not achieved something worthwhile. [11]My folks _____ all given up on me, but I _____ not. [12]Someday, I will find what I _____ always been looking for, and I will be successful too.

EXERCISE 2.1-C   *Write* have *or* has, *whichever is correct, in the blanks.*

A BOOK OF WORLD RECORDS

[1]For the past several years, a book of world records _____ been published. [2]So many people _____ bought it that it _____ become a best seller. [3]Writing the book _____ not been easy for the authors. [4]They _____ been careful to include only authenticated records, although authenticating the records _____ at times been difficult. [5]Many people _____ tried to get their names in the book, but only a few _____ succeeded.

[6]If you _____ ever read the book, you will know that it contains some very unusual records. [7]One man whose name appears in the book _____ surmounted the problems of playing a violin under water and gives concerts from a swimming pool. [8]The English language _____ made it into the book by having the largest vocabulary—490,000 words plus another 300,000 technical terms. [9]One man _____ walked from Vienna to Paris–a distance of 871 miles–on his hands! [10]Another _____ pulled a locomotive and a truck weighing 135.5 tons with his teeth! [11]An Australian man took a shower that lasted 202 hours and an English woman rocked in a rocking chair for 432

hours. ¹²An English man ＿＿＿＿＿ attended 4,160 theatrical productions in
20 years of theatre going and is still going. ¹³There ＿＿＿＿＿ never been a
record-breaker like Jesse Owens, who broke six world records on a single day in
1935. ¹⁴So many people ＿＿＿＿＿ bought the record book that the book itself
＿＿＿＿＿ claimed an enviable record as the fastest-selling book in the world.

3. Subject/Aux-Word Agreement (Past Tense)

3.1   The forms of aux-words indicate time—present and past. There are two past tense
forms of *be: was* and *were. Was* is used with singular, noncount, and *-ing* verb form
subjects. Nevertheless, *was* is **not** used when the subject is the pronoun *you. Were*
is used with plural subjects and the pronoun *you.*

> I *was* studying English.
> My sister *was* studying English.
> Much dedication *was* necessary.
> Studying English *was* a challenge.
> My friends *were* studying English.
> You *were* studying English.

3.2   Except for the forms of *be* (*is, am, are*), all aux-words have only one past tense
form.

Present	Past
have, has	*had*
do, does	*did*
can	*could*
will	*would*
may	*might*
shall	*should*
must	(*Must* has no past form. *Had to* is used to show past necessity.)

Present	Past
Joe *has* done his homework The other students *have* done their homework.	Joe *had* done his homework. The other students *had* done their homework.
I *don't* know the answer. My friend *doesn't* know the answer.	I *didn't* know the answer. My friend *didn't* know the answer.

EXERCISE 3-A   *Rewrite the following paragraph substituting* In 1895 *for* Now. *You will have to change
the aux-words to agree with this new time.*

PASSENGER PIGEONS

¹Now we are crossing the great plains of North America. ²Thousands of birds
are seen daily. ³The greatest flocks are the passenger pigeons, numbering in the
thousands. ⁴They are different from the birds back home as their tails are longer

than their wings. [5]These birds don't fly high beyond our reach. [6]Instead, the huge flocks are right above our heads. [7]Everyone is very excited about shooting them because one doesn't have to be a good marksman to hit these targets. [8]Anyone can shoot down a bird or two with every shot. [9]Sometimes we will kill hundreds in a day.[10]I don't think we will ever see the end of the passenger pigeon.

EXERCISE 3-B   *Rewrite the following paragraphs substituting* Many years ago *for* Today. *You will have to change the aux-words to agree with this new time.*

THE SAMOAN MATAI*

[1]Today in Samoa matais are very powerful. [2]They are able to decide for the entire family or village. [3]They do not have to consult others in making decisions. [4]They can assign anyone to do certain tasks. [5]They can collect wages.

[6]However, being a matai is also a responsibility. [7]A matai is expected to provide for his family or village. [8]He is responsible for the welfare of everyone under his leadership.

[9]Matais are elected by the family. [10]The top village matai is usually elected by the family matais. [11]Once elected, a matai is usually a matai for life.

*Matai = Chief

EXERCISE 3-C   *Rewrite the following paragraph substituting* One of the older materials *for* One of today's materials. *You will have to change the aux-words to agree with this new time.*

TAPA CLOTH

[1]One of today's materials is tapa cloth, which is a fabric made from trees. [2]It is used for clothing and bedding by many people on South Pacific islands. [3]Thin strips of bark from the paper mulberry tree are pounded into 18-inch-wide strips. [4]These strips are glued together with paste made from the tapioca root. [5]The material can then be painted with dyes which are made from other plants. [6]The resulting material can be fashioned into clothes or bedding. [7]It is warm and quite durable. [8]One drawback of tapa cloth, however, is that it cannot be washed with water. [9]It can only be put in the sun or aired to clean it.

4. Yes/No Questions and Aux-Words

4.1   Aux-words are used for many important purposes. For instance, (as pictured on page 53), they are needed to form:

- yes/no questions (questions that are answered *yes* or *no*),
- negative statements or questions, and
- emphatic statements.

Aux-words are also used with tag and *wh-* questions (explained in Chapter 7, section 11) and as predicate substitutes (explained in Chapter 9, section 3).

4.2   Yes/No questions are questions that can be answered with *yes* or *no*. To change a simple statement into a written yes/no question,

1. find the aux-word (if there is no apparent aux-word, it may be "hidden"; see the following section) and
2. move the aux-word to the front of the sentence. (If the aux-word is a contraction, such as *don't*, you may "un-contract" it and then move only the aux-word. But be careful! Sometimes this process changes—even reverses—the meaning.)

Don Quixote **was** a dreamer.   (aux-word = *was*)

Was Don Quixote   a dreamer?

He couldn't really change the world.   (aux-word = *couldn't*)

Couldn't he   really change the world?   OR   **Could** he **not** really change the world?

4.3   The process of moving the aux-word to change a statement into a yes/no question indicates the complete subject of the sentence. The word/words between the first (statement) aux-word position and the second (question) aux-word position are the subject.

Christmas **is** coming soon.

Is Christmas   coming soon?   (subject = Christmas)

The brown packages lying on the table **are** ready to be mailed.

Are the brown packages lying on the table   ready to be mailed?
                (subject = the brown packages lying on the table)

The decorations, tinsel, and bright lights for the tree **have** been unpacked.

Have the decorations, tinsel, and bright lights for the tree   been unpacked?
                (subject = the decorations, tinsel, and bright lights for the tree)

EXERCISE 4-A   *Rewrite each of the following affirmative sentences into a* yes/no *question by moving the aux-word from its position after the subject to a position in front of the subject.*

SHARKS—PART I

1. A shark's primary food is fish, sea turtles, birds, and other sharks.

2. They will feed on almost anything found in the sea.

3. Most sharks are dangerous to man.

4. They will attack without warning.

5. The great white shark is the most famous man-eater.

6. It is always hungry and never afraid.

7. Its razor-sharp, triangular teeth can slice through anything.

8. Sharks can grow new teeth if they lose them.

9. Fishermen don't usually catch sharks for food.

10. The number of sharks has increased in the past twenty or thirty years.

EXERCISE 4-B   *Rewrite each of the following affirmative sentences into a* yes/no *question by moving the aux-word from its position after the subject to a position in front of the subject.*

SHARKS—PART II

1. The tiger shark is the most common of the sharks.

2. It is normally a slow swimmer.

3. It is very fast when chasing something.

4. Tiger sharks have frequently been seen in shallow water.

5. They have sometimes attacked men.

6. They do not seem to need a reason.

7. Many strange things have been found in sharks' stomachs.

8. They will eat anything.

9. A roll of roofing paper was once found in a tiger shark's stomach.

10. There was also a keg of nails.

11. Sharks can be of use to man.

12. Fine leather can be made from tiger shark skin.

13. The oil from the liver is also valuable.

EXERCISE 4-C   *Rewrite each of the following affirmative sentences into a* yes/no *question by moving the aux-word from its position after the subject to a position in front of the subject.*

SHARKS—PART III

1. Men have been seeking a shark repellent for a long time.

2. Many things have been tried.

3. These have included mechanical, electrical, and chemical devices.

4. What works on one shark does not always work on another.

5. Shark nets are used to keep sharks away from bathing beaches in Australia and South Africa.

6. The sharks are caught in the net by their gills as they swim toward the shore.

7. Shark fisheries have reduced the number of sharks in some areas.

8. The most effective control of sharks would be to catch them.

9. Sharks could be used for food.

10. They could also be used for fertilizer, oil, leather, and many other things.

11. Sharks would then be benefactors of man instead of his enemies.

5. Hidden Aux-Words

Some statements have no apparent aux-word. The aux-word is hidden within the time-included verb form. (Time-included and timeless verb forms are explained in Chapter 5.) However, this aux-word comes out of hiding when it is needed to form a question or a negative.

A simple way to understand hidden aux-words is to compare them to three mice named Do, Does, and Did.* Does and Did have long curly tails, but Do has no tail.

*Adapted from Robert L. Allen's " 'The Mice': Do, Does, and Did" in *English Teaching Forum* (Vol. 12, No.2, April–June 1974, pp. 13–17).

When they find a large piece of cheese (a verb), these three mice dig right into it until they are hidden inside. However, they leave their long tails outside of the cheese. In the pictures below, you can see Did's and Does's tails. Of course, Do has no tail, so it doesn't show.

Those boys **play** all day.

That girl **smiles** at everyone.

They **lived** in that house a long time.

When a cat (a question) comes along, the mice (aux-words) get as far away from it as they can, so they leave the cheese (verb) and move to the other side of the subject. Of course, their tails go with them, and when the mice are outside of the cheese, they are no longer hidden.

do those boys **play** all day ?

does that girl **smile** at everyone ?

did they **live** in that house a long time ?

In more sophisticated terms, to form a yes/no question from these statements, the hidden aux-word (*do*, *does*, or *did*) must be taken out and moved to the front of the sentence. The time-included form then changes to the timeless base form.

The student **goes** to school every day.	The student **studied** English last year.
Does the student **go** to school every day?	**Did** the student **study** English last year?
The students **go** to school every day.	The students **studied** English last year.
Do the students **go** to school every day?	**Did** the students **study** English last year?

EXERCISE 5-A   *Rewrite each of the following affirmative sentences into a question by moving the aux-word to a position in front of the subject. You will have to supply the hidden aux-words.*

EARLY AGRICULTURE

1. People of earlier times wandered from place to place to find food.

2. Some members of these wandering tribes finally decided to plant grain seeds.

3. They stayed in one place.

4. They raised only a few kinds of crops.

5. Explorers traveled to new lands.

6. They found many different kinds of food.

7. They took seeds and roots home with them.

8. The people planted these.

9. The new foods enlarged their diet.

10. This variety in their diets made them healthier.

11. We know the importance of a well-balanced diet nowadays.

12. Eating a variety of foods also makes life more interesting and enjoyable.

EXERCISE 5-B   *Rewrite each of the following affirmative sentences into a question by moving the aux-word to a position in front of the subject. You will have to supply the hidden aux-words.*

HOLIDAYS

1. Everyone enjoys a holiday.

2. Holidays commemorate religious or political events, and national or international occasions.

3. Many cultures share holidays.

4. Others relate to only one culture.

5. People use different calendars.

6. They even celebrate the new year at different times.

7. Many countries have some sort of harvest holiday.

8. The United States has Thanksgiving.

9. Ancient Hawaiians observed the Makahiki.

10. Independence initiated many in-country holidays.

11. The United States celebrates the Fourth of July.

12. Korea's independence day occurs on August 15th.

EXERCISE 5-C   *Rewrite each of the following affirmative sentences into a question by moving the aux-word to a position in front of the subject. You will have to supply the hidden aux-words.*

POLLUTION

1. Many people suffer from respiratory diseases.

2. Smog contributes to their discomfort.

3. Air pollution aggravates their condition.

4. Government agencies monitor pollution levels.

5. Some cities broadcast smog alerts.

6. This warns people to stay indoors and limit their physical activity.

7. Federal and state government laws prohibit excess pollution.

8. Automobile exhaust contaminates the air.

9. Automobile emissions standards help control this problem.

10. Heavy industry pollutes the environment.

11. The elimination of pollutants from this source increases production costs.

12. The health advantages of a clean environment outweigh these economic disadvantages.

EXERCISE 5.1-A   *Rewrite each of the following affirmative sentences into a* yes/no *question by moving the aux-word to a position in front of the subject. In some sentences you will have to supply the hidden aux-words.*

MARY'S ENGLISH

1. Mary is a college student this semester.

2. She speaks a little English.

3. She has trouble writing it.

4. She is interested in improving her English skills.

5. She has enrolled in an intensive English program.

6. She doesn't take any other classes.

7. Mary plans on enrolling in other classes later.

8. There are many other students like Mary in the English program.

9. They work hard to learn to write English.

10. They may also take typing classes.

11. The diligent ones will eventually master English.

12. They can then take classes in their major fields.

EXERCISE 5.1-B   *Rewrite each of the following affirmative sentences into a* yes/no *question by moving the aux-word to a position in front of the subject. In some sentences you will have to supply the hidden aux-words.*

THE HOLIDAY SEASON

1. Christmas is always fun.

2. We spend Christmas Eve singing Christmas carols.

3. Favorite stories are repeated year after year.

4. Family members don't have to work or go to school.

5. Christmas dinner is a festive meal.

6. There is always lots of special food.

7. We spend the holiday season visiting friends and relatives.

8. New Year's Day comes one week later.

9. Everyone celebrates New Year's Eve.

10. There are many parties.

11. There is lots of good food and drink.

12. People make resolutions that are never kept.

13. The holiday season seems to be over too soon.

14. We are always sad to see these holidays end.

EXERCISE 5.1-C   *Rewrite each of the following affirmative sentences into a* yes/no *question by moving the aux-word to a position in front of the subject. In some sentences you will have to supply the hidden aux-words.*

THIS CLASS

1. The students in this class come from many different backgrounds.

2. Some of them grew up in this area.

3. Others have recently moved here from far away.

4. They all need to improve their writing skills.

5. Most of them try hard in class.

6. They complete all their assignments conscientiously.

7. They think about what they are doing.

8. A few of them do not understand the true purpose of the class.

9. These students fail to realize that the class is designed to help them.

10. They continually fight against it.

11. One tries to think of ways to get out of doing the homework.

12. Another cheats on the tests.

13. These students don't realize that they are only cheating themselves.

14. The real test is whether or not their writing improves to an acceptable level.

15. Writing correctly in many different situations and at various different times will be the true exam.

16. This test will face them many times in life long after this class is finished.

6. Negatives and Aux-Words

All negative sentences using *not* require an aux-word. The aux-word may precede the *not* or combine with it in a contraction.

When an affirmative statement contains only a hidden aux-word, that aux-word (*do, does,* or *did*) must appear before the *not* in the corresponding negative statement.

EXAMPLE:

John works hard.
John **does not** work hard.

When making a yes/no question from a negative statement with an aux-word and *not,* only the aux-word moves to the new position in front of the subject.

EXAMPLE:

John **will not** fail this class.
Will John   **not** fail this class?

However, when the aux-word is contracted with the *not,* the entire unit is moved to the new position in front of the subject.

EXAMPLE

John **won't** fail this class.
Won't John   fail this class?

Both of these examples have the same meaning. However, the contracted form is less formal. (Writing is usually more formal than speech.)

EXERCISE 6-A

Rewrite the following affirmative sentences as negative sentences. You will have to supply the hidden aux-word. Your new title will be "John is not an A Student." Your first sentence will be "John's teachers do not enjoy having him in class."

JOHN IS AN A STUDENT

[1]John's teachers enjoy having him in class. [2]He comes to class on time. [3]He listens intently to the instructor. [4]He wants to learn. [5]He passes all the tests. [6]His work habits evidence his sincerity. [7]He reads the assignments. [8]He completes his homework every night. [9]John listens to the laboratory tapes. [10]He does extra work. [11]He learns English rapidly. [12]Other students emulate his example. [13]John speaks only English on campus.

EXERCISE 6-B

Rewrite the following affirmative sentences as negative sentences. You will have to supply the hidden aux-word in some of the sentences. Your new title will be "Good Students." Your first sentence will be "Robin and Terry are not bad students."

BAD STUDENTS

[1]Robin and Terry are bad students. [2]They arrive late very often. [3]They sit in the back of the classroom. [4]They talk when they should be listening. [5]They sleep during the teacher's presentations. [6]Their notebooks are filled with doodles. [7]They do sloppy work. [8]They forget to do their assignments. [9]They misunderstand instructions. [10]They do things the wrong way. [11]They blame others when they have problems. [12]They complain about the work they have to do.

EXERCISE 6-C   *Rewrite the following affirmative sentences as negative sentences. You will have to supply the hidden aux-word in some of the sentences. Your first sentence will be "Money is not a necessary commodity."*

MONEY

[1]Money is a necessary commodity. [2]People in all countries use it. [3]It is impossible to carry on trade without it. [4]Industry would come to a standstill without money. [5]Business would collapse. [6]Money needs to be regulated. [7]It is necessary to have banks to regulate money. [8]Financial institutions bring prosperity. [9]Bank failures cause hard times. [10]The world revolves fundamentally on bank credit. [11]Having an international currency seems desirable. [12]This would ensure world-wide prosperity.

7. Verb/Aux-Word Look-Alikes

7.1   Some aux-words and verbs look alike, but they do not have the same function or meaning. They should not be confused.

Aux-Word		Verb	
Present	Past	Present	Past
do, does	*did*	*do, does*	*did*
have, has	*had*	*have, has*	*had*
can	*could*	*can*	*canned*
will	*would*	*will*	*willed*

7.2   Like all verbs, these verbs have hidden aux-words that must be used* when making yes/no questions and negatives.

John does his homework every day.	Does John do his homework every day? John doesn't do his homework every day.
John and Mary do their homework together.	Do John and Mary do their homework together? John and Mary don't do their homework together.
John did his homework last night.	Did John do his homework last night? John didn't do his homework last night.
John has a new car.	Does John have a new car? John doesn't have a new car.
John and Mary have a new car.	Do John and Mary have a new car? John and Mary don't have a new car.
John had an old car.	Did John have an old car? John didn't have an old car.
Mary cans tomatoes every summer.	Does Mary can tomatoes every summer? Mary doesn't can tomatoes every summer.
Mary canned tomatoes last summer.**	Did Mary can tomatoes last summer? Mary didn't can tomatoes last summer.
He willed his property to the Red Cross.***	Did he will his property to the Red Cross? He didn't will his property to the Red Cross.

*Instead of using the hidden aux-word, British English commonly uses the entire verb *have,* as in the nursery rhyme "Baa, baa, black sheep, have you any wool?" and the negative reply "I haven't any."
**The verb *can* means "preserve in cans or bottles." British English uses the verb *tin.*
***The verb *will* means "leave to someone or endow." An older meaning of the verb *will* is *want,* e.g., "The Lord's obedient children do what He wills." As a verb, *will* is rarely used in the present tense.

7.3   These verbs and aux-words may be used together.

> *Do* you *do* it this way?
> He *had had* dinner before he came.
> She˙*can can* fruit tomorrow.
> He *will will* his money to us.

8. Modal Aux-Words

The aux-words *is, am, are, was,* and *were* establish a **connection** or linkage between the subject and the complement that follows (Complements are explained in Chapter 7, section 9). They are also used with *-ing* verb forms to indicate activity in progress (Chapter 6, section 5) and with *d-t-n* forms to create a passive construction (Chapter 10).

The aux-words *have, has,* and *had* indicate activity or state of being that occurred at an **earlier time** (Chapter 6, section 6).

The aux-words *do, does,* and *did* are used in **question** or **negative formation** when there is no other aux-word (sections 5 and 6 of this chapter). They are also used to create **emphasis** and/or as **verb-substitutes** in affirmative statements.

> "*Do* you care about passing this class?"
> "Oh, yes, I really *do* want to pass it!"
> "He *doesn't* look very intelligent."
> "Don't let his looks fool you. He *is.*"

In contrast, the **modal aux-words** indicate a wide variety of different meanings. Most of them have present and past forms that show time. Nevertheless, in addition to showing time, these forms also indicate additional meanings and functions:

- Later (future) time
- Repeated action in the past
- Prediction/Probability/Possibility
- Ability
- Necessity/Obligation
- Advisability
- Permission
- Request
- Suggestion
- Preference

The same modal aux-word form may be used to indicate several different meanings or functions. The correct (intended) one must often be determined from the meaning of the context (the words before and after it).

8.1   **TIME LATER THAN THE TENSE EXPRESSED**
Later time in the present (often called future time) is expressed by the modals *will* and *shall.* (Expressions with *going to* after an appropriate *be* aux-word are also used to show later time.)

> I haven't read the book, but I *shall* read it.
> I haven't read the book, but I *will* read it.
> (I haven't read the book, but I *am going to* read it.)

(Some grammars have prescribed the use of *shall* with *I* and *we*, and *will* with other pronouns. In reality, *will* is used with all subject pronouns, and *shall* is most commonly used for making suggestions and extending invitations. [See section 8.9])

Later time in the past (i.e., time later than that expressed by a main, past-tense verb) is indicated by the modal *would* (expressions with *going to* also show later time in the past).

> He said that he hadn't read the book but he *would* read it.
> (He said that he hadn't read the book but he *was going to* read it.)

8.2 REPEATED ACTION IN THE PAST

The modal *would* is also used to indicate past action that was habitual or customary (Another way of expressing this same idea is to use the expression *used to*. [See Chapter 6, section 4.2.])

> When we were young, we *would* swim in the river every day during summer vacation.
> (When I was a boy, I *used to* earn money by shoveling snow in the winter.)

8.3 PREDICTION/PROBABILITY/POSSIBILITY

The modals *will, must, should, ought to, may, might,* and *could* are all used to predict the possibility of an action. However, they indicate different degrees of probability.

Definite plans and/or certainty are indicated with the modal *will.*

> I *will* be there Saturday morning. You can count on me.
> Something *will* turn up. I'm sure of it.

The **strong probability** of a **logical conclusion** (based on evidence) is indicated with the modal *must.*

> That man looks Oriental, and he is speaking Korean. He *must* be a Korean.
> It is January, and you are in Alaska. It *must* be cold where you are.

Strong probability is also indicated with *should* or *ought to.*

> Alice *should* do well on that test. She's a bright woman.
> George *ought to* do well on that test. He has studied hard.

Possibility (but not strong probability) is indicated with *may, might, can*, or *could*.

> Something *may* turn up. I hope so anyway.
> Something *might* turn up. You never know.
> It *can* get cold in the mountains, even during the summer.
> It *could* get cold tonight. You might need an extra blanket.

Weak possibility (usually in an *if* clause) is expressed with *should*.

> I've waited long enough. I'm leaving. If he *should* come, tell him I left.

8.4 ABILITY

Can is used to indicate present ability. *Could* is used to indicate past ability. (Another way of expressing this idea is to use the expression *able to* after a *be* aux-word.)

> Bill *can* swim now. (That class he took really helped!)
> He *could* not swim last year. (He would drown if he fell in the water.)
> (Bill is *able to* swim now, but last year he was not *able to* swim at all.)

8.5 NECESSITY/OBLIGATION

Must is the modal that expresses the idea that something is mandatory (or at least extremely important or strongly recommended). It usually indicates that there is no alternative. (Another way of indicating this meaning is to use the expression *have to*.)

> You *must* do your homework or you will fail this class.
> (You *have to* do your homework or you will fail this class.)
> You really *must* meet my husband. You two have a lot in common.

Musn't (the negative form of *must*) does *not* indicate that something is not necessary. It carries the meaning of *prohibition*.

> You *mustn't* wipe your dirty hands on the tablecloth. Doing that is
>   very rude.

The real opposite of *must* is the negative form of *have to*. It means that something is not necessary.

> You *don't have to* do that assignment. The teacher said it is optional.

8.6 ADVISABILITY

The modal *should* or *ought to* is used to show that a course of action is strongly recommended but not absolutely necessary.

> Take my advice. You *should* study more and play around less.
> If you're feeling sick, you *ought to* go home and rest.

When advice is more of a **warning** (especially if there is a **threat of bad results** if the advice/warning is not followed), the appropriate modal expression is *had better*. In speaking and informal writing, this expression usually becomes *'d better*.

> You had better get out of here before the police arrive.
> I'd better go home right now or my father will be very angry.

8.7 PERMISSION

The modal *may* is used to ask for or give permission. (*Can*, though frequently used for asking permission in speech, is too informal for this purpose in most types of written English.)

> May I leave?
> Yes, you may leave now.

8.8 REQUEST

To ask for something (assistance, permission, etc.), a number of different modal aux-words are used: *may, will, could, would, can* (informal), and *might* (rare).

> May I borrow your pencil, please?
> Will you please help me lift this table?
> Could you please lend me your pen?
> Hey, Joe, can you help me with my homework?

8.9 SUGGESTION/INVITATION

The modal *could* is often used (in present tense) to make a suggestion. Likewise, questions with *shall* are often used to make a suggestion or to extend an invitation.

> If you need help, you could talk to your teacher.
> Shall we turn on the air conditioning?
> Shall we dance?
> Shall we go now?

8.10 PREFERENCE

The two-word aux-word *would rather* is used to indicate preference. In speaking and informal writing, *would rather* if often contracted to *'d rather*.

> Mr. Smith would rather see you later this afternoon. Can you come at 3:00?
> On days like this, I'd rather be at the beach than in the library.

EXERCISE 8-A   *Supply the appropriate aux-word in each of the blanks. Choose an aux-word that shows the meaning or function indicated in parentheses under the blank.*

LEARNING ENGLISH

[1]Many students learning English take classes so that they _____
(ability)

learn to communicate in English. [2]The teacher _____ help the
(possibility)

students learn, but he or she _____ not learn for them. [3]Each student
(ability)

_____ do his own work. [4]He, himself, _____ learn to speak,
(necessity)   (necessity)

read, and write English. [5]Some students _____ unaware of this fact,
(connection)

or if aware of it, forget it. [6]They _____ try anything to avoid doing
(later time)

their assignments. [7]They _____ say they want to learn English, but
(possibility)

their actions _____ not support their words.
(negative formation)

EXERCISE 8-B   *Supply the appropriate aux-word in each of the blanks. Choose an aux-word that shows the meaning or function indicated in parentheses under the blank. There is more than one possible answer for some blanks.*

HISTORY

[1]History _____ a fascinating subject. [2]Everyone _____
(connection)   (advisability)

have a knowledge of history. [3]When you study history, you _____
(later time)

learn many important things. [4]Understanding the past _____ help you
(ability)

understand the present. [5]A thorough knowledge of the past _____
(possibility)

even allow you to predict the future.

[6]The subject matter of history _____ as diverse as the people
(connection)

and places of the world. [7]The study of history _____ the study of
(connection)

the foundation, growth, and decline of civilization. [8]A complete historical

view _____ include major intellectual, artistic, social, and spiritual
(necessity)

contributions of the period and people studied.

[9]A general overview of world history _____ give you ideas
(possibility)

of specific areas you _____ want to study. [10]If you study one
(possibility)

of these areas in depth you _____ become a specialist. [11]You
(possibility)

_____ choose a specific time period or geographical area to study.
(advisability)

¹²You ＿＿＿＿＿＿＿ specialize in medieval Europe. ¹³Polynesian history
(possibility)

＿＿＿＿＿＿＿ interest you. ¹⁴You ＿＿＿＿＿＿＿ be fascinated by ancient
(possibility)   (possibility)

China. ¹⁵The history of many groups ＿＿＿＿＿＿＿ never been written
(earlier time)

down. ¹⁶If you convert oral histories to writing, you ＿＿＿＿＿＿＿ make a
(possibility)

contribution to world knowledge.

¹⁷Whatever area or period you choose, you ＿＿＿＿＿＿＿ need supporting
(later time)

skills to be a successful historian. ¹⁸The ability to read and write well in English

and other languages ＿＿＿＿＿＿＿ an important prerequisite to serious
(connection)

historical study.

EXERCISE 8-C   *Supply the appropriate aux-word in each of the blanks. Choose an aux-word that shows the meaning or function indicated in parentheses under the blank. There is more than one possible answer for some blanks.*

LATIN AMERICA

¹Latin America ＿＿＿＿＿＿＿ a region filled with contrast and variety. ²Vast
(connection)

jungles, forbidding mountains, dry deserts, and endless plains ＿＿＿＿＿＿＿
(connection)

all part of its varied geography. ³A broad variety of climatic conditions

＿＿＿＿＿＿＿ be encountered in Latin America.
(ability)

⁴Even in the area of language, Latin America ＿＿＿＿＿＿＿ diverse. ⁵All
(connection)

Latin Americans ＿＿＿＿＿＿＿ not speak Spanish. ⁶Portuguese, French,
(negative formation)

Dutch, and English ＿＿＿＿＿＿＿ some of the other languages spoken in the
(connection)

many different countries of Latin America.

⁷The countries of Latin America ＿＿＿＿＿＿＿ not consider themselves
(negative formation)

similar. ⁸Rivalry between countries ＿＿＿＿＿＿＿ not uncommon. ⁹Each
(connection)

country ＿＿＿＿＿＿＿ developed its own solutions. ¹⁰Many different kinds
(earlier time)

of governments ＿＿＿＿＿＿＿ be found in Latin America. ¹¹Both left-wing
(ability)

and right-wing dictatorships ＿＿＿＿＿＿＿ found. ¹²There ＿＿＿＿＿＿＿
(connection)   (connection)

a growing middle ground in politics. ¹³Stable, moderate governments

＿＿＿＿＿＿＿ common. ¹⁴The social middle class ＿＿＿＿＿＿＿ also grown
(connection)   (earlier time)

considerably in recent years.

[15]Rapid change _____ apparent throughout Latin America. [16]Busy
                        (connection)

ports and industrial centers _____ be seen in most Latin American
                                  (ability)

countries. [17]Exports from Latin America are growing and _____
                                                              (later time)

continue to grow in the future. [18]North Americans _____ understand
                                                       (advisabililty)

this important part of the world better.

EXERCISE 8.1-A   *Supply the appropriate aux-word in each of the blanks. Choose an aux-word that shows
the meaning or function indicated in parentheses under the blank. There is more than
one possible answer for some blanks.*

A BUSY LIFE

[1]Sometimes I _____ not know what to do. [2]The problem
                   (negative formation)

_____ not that I _____ not have anything to occupy my
   (connection)   (negative formation)

time. [3]Rather, I have too many things to do. [4]There _____ just too
                                                            (connection)

many demands on my time. [5]The first thing in the morning, I plan my day. [6]I

look at my "to do" list from yesterday and cross off the things I _____
                                                                      (earlier time)

already done. [7]Then I look at what is left and decide what I _____
                                                                   (later time)

do today. [8]There are some things I simply _____ do. [9]They take
                                                (necessity)

top priority. [10]I decide when I _____ do them. [11]Then, in the time
                                      (later time)

periods that _____ left, I schedule the things I _____ do,
                 (connection)   (advisability)

even though they _____ not first priority. [12]Finally, I remember
                     (connection)

that I _____ schedule some things that I like to do, to keep myself
           (advisability)

from burning out. [13]Of course, those activities _____ not nearly as
                                                       (connection)

enjoyable when they are precisely scheduled. [14]At last, my day _____
                                                                     (connection)

all planned from morning until evening. [15]That's when my mother asks,

"_____ you help me clean out the garage today?" [16]Then my
     (request)

little brother pleads, "_____ you please fix my bike?" [17]How
                            (request)

_____ I refuse them? [18]Sometimes I wonder why I even go to the
   (ability)

trouble of planning my day. [19]I _____ just get up early and go fishing
                                      (preference)

to get away from it all.

EXERCISE 8.1-B   *Supply the appropriate aux-word in each of the blanks. Choose an aux-word that shows the meaning or function indicated in parentheses under the blank. There is more than one possible answer for some blanks.*

ACADEMIC ADVISEMENT

[1]Yesterday I went to see my academic advisor. [2]I needed her signature so I

_____ add a class. [3]I _____ not realize the process would be
    (ability)   (negative formation)

so involved.

   [4]First, I asked, "_____ I take this class?"
                     (permission)

   [5]She responded, "You not only _____, you _____."
                                (permission)   (necessity)

   [6]"_____ I take it this semester?"
       (ability)

   [7]"Well," she replied, "you _____, but you don't have to."
                         (possibility)

   [8]"What _____ the alternatives?" I wondered.
            (connection)

   [9]"You _____ wait until next semester, that might be better,
          (suggestion)

or—now that I think about it—you _____ take another class as a
                            (suggestion)

substitution. [10]You _____ want to do that if one of the substitute
                 (possibility)

courses _____ more interesting to you."
      (connection)

   [11]"I think I _____ take this course now and get it over with," I
              (preference)

replied.

   [12]Instead of signing my form, she gave me more advice. [13]"When I

_____ a freshman, I had the same attitude. [14]I just wanted to get
    (connection)

through school. [15]I _____ take any class that was required without
          (repeated action in past)

even thinking about the other possibilities and my own interests. [16]Little did I

realize what I was missing. [17]Pretty soon I started to hate school. [18]Why, I had

one teacher..."

   [19]"_____ we get back on the subject?" I asked.
       (invitation)

   [20]"What _____ that?"
         (connection)

   [21]"I need you to sign this paper for me."

   [22]"Oh yes, of course," she said, and scratched her initials on the form.

   [23]"Thanks a lot!" I said as I moved toward the door. [24]I _____
                                               (later time)

always remember your advice."

EXERCISE 8.1-C   *Supply the appropriate aux-word in each of the blanks. Choose an aux-word that shows the meaning or function indicated in parentheses under the blank. There is more than one possible answer for some blanks.*

COMPUTER REVOLUTION

[1]When I _____ young, if I wanted to write something, I
(connection)

_____ get out a pencil and a piece of paper. [2]Later, I graduated
(repeated action in past)

to a pen, but my writing instrument needs _____ still simple.
(connection)

[3]As I got older, I learned that the ability to type _____ help me
(later time)

in almost any career I chose. [4]Therefore, in high school I enrolled in a typing

class even though I _____ have taken art or shop. [5]Learning to
(preference)

type _____ not easy. [6]The teacher was constantly harping, "Now
(connection)

students, you _____ look at your fingers while you type." [7]But if I
(prohibition)

_____ not look at my fingers, I _____ not tell which keys to
(negative formation)   (ability)

press. [8]It nearly drove me crazy!

[9]My investment of time and energy in learning to type, however,

_____ pay off eventually. [10]The keyboard skills I developed proved
(emphasis)

especially useful when the office where I worked became computerized. [11]Once

that happened, nearly everything I wrote had to be typed.

[12]Now, I have a different problem. [13]If I want to write something, I

_____ choose which word processor to use. [14]There are dozens
(necessity)

of them and each one has its own secrets that _____ be learned!
(necessity)

[15]Likewise, if I want to add up a column of figures, I need to use a

computerized spreadsheet. [16]Once again, I _____ invest time in
(necessity)

learning how to operate the program. [17]Even drawing a simple picture requires

special "paint" software. [18]Things that used to be simple have become quite

complicated. [19]More than ever, there _____ things that drive me crazy.
(connection)

[20]The computer revolution _____ not necessarily made things easier
(earlier time)

for me.

9. Proofreading

As explained previously, an important part of the process of writing is proofreading. Although you now have a better understanding of aux-words and how they are used, you may still make occasional mistakes with them.

The following exercises will give you practice in focused proofreading. The passages contain numerous mistakes with aux-words, but that is the only type of error they contain. Using what you have learned in this chapter, focus on finding and fixing the incorrect aux-words.

EXERCISE 9-A

In the paragraphs below, there are a number of errors involving aux-words (lack of agreement with the subject, non-use when necessary, or wrong choice). Find the errors, correct them, and then rewrite the passage. Do not add, remove, or change any words except aux-words and accompanying verb forms.

LASERS—PART I

[1]For nearly a century, science-fiction tales has been told about aliens from outer space armed with mysterious ray guns. [2]These guns, which is capable of shooting powerful beams of heat and light, must vaporize earthlings instantly and should burn through wood doors and melt through metal walls like a hot knife cutting through butter.

[3]Today, however, such "swords of heat" is a reality. [4]They are lasers, narrow beams of the most intense light ever known. [5]Some of them burn more intensely than the light at the surface of the sun. [6]Do you imagine that? [7]These lasers shall indeed melt through metal and vaporize solid objects.

[8]Of course, most uses for laser light is much more peaceful and useful. [9]For example, art detectives do use laser microprobes to test the authenticity of old paintings. [10]You wonder how they do that? [11]Well, the laser is used to vaporize a tiny amount (about a millionth of an ounce) of the paint, and the vaporized material are analyzed. [12]The results of this analysis is compared with what is known about old paints. [13]For example, most modern oil paints contain zinc, but paint makers not use zinc before 1820. [14]If the material vaporized by the laser contains zinc, the art detective must know that the "old" painting is a fake.

EXERCISE 9-B

In the paragraphs below, there are a number of errors involving aux-words (lack of agreement with the subject, non-use when necessary, or wrong choice). Find the errors, correct them, and then rewrite the passage. Do not add, remove, or change any words except aux-words and accompanying verb forms.

LASERS—PART II

[1]Do lasers can be used for other useful purposes? [2]Of course! [3]In fact, there do not seem to be any limit to the ways lasers could be used.

[4]Lasers are valuable for many industrial purposes. [5]For example, one company now does use a ruby laser to pierce tiny holes in diamonds. [6]Very thin copper wire, the diameter of a human hair, might then be drawn through the hole. [7]The company does produce 30 million miles of this wire each year. [8]In the process, it wears out (and must replace) thousands of diamonds. [9]Since diamond are the hardest material in the world, making holes in diamonds are quite difficult and time consuming. [10]Using traditional methods, the piercing process did used to take two days. [11]A laser must do the same job in a few minutes. [12]Can you believe that?

[13]Another important use of lasers are in medicine. [14]Laser light is used to burn away cancerous growths on the skin. [15]Stronger laser beams can be used as "bloodless" scalpels, since they cut and cauterize (burn the flesh and stop the bleeding)

at the same time. [16]Strangely enough, this procedure is not very painful, the pain does last only a moment, and there are no pain afterward. [17]One patient said it felt like a drop of hot candle wax falling on his skin.

EXERCISE 9-C   *In the paragraphs below, there are a number of errors involving aux-words (lack of agreement with the subject, non-use when necessary, or wrong choice). Find the errors, correct them, and then rewrite the passage. Do not add, remove, or change any words except aux-words and accompanying verb forms.*

LASERS—PART III

[1]Laser light is very powerful and should be blinding. [2]For this reason, technicians working with lasers often wear dark goggles to protect their eyes. [3]Even reflected laser rays should burn holes in the retina (the back, inner lining of the eye), and the retina might be in flawless condition or else some vision will be lost.

[4]Strangely enough, however, laser instruments are also used to repair retinas which has been damaged. [5]Various injuries shall cause the retina to become torn or detatched from the back of the eye. [6]If this damage not repaired, imperfect vision or even blindness should result. [7]Nevertheless, using traditional surgical methods with the delicate retina is very difficult for the surgeon and risky for the patient. [8]With lasers, the procedure are much easier. [9]The patient sits in a chair and does tilt his/her head until the retina falls into the right position. [10]The doctor then picks up a small laser instrument and aims it through the pupil of the eye at the torn edges in the retina. [11]The instrument flashes weak laser pulses on the retina and burns a series of tiny scars around the torn edge. [12]These scars not injure the eye. [13]Rather, they "weld" the torn retina back in place. [14]Isn't that amazing?

[15]As you might see, lasers no longer science fiction. [16]They widely used in the reality which each of us does live in. [17]Nowadays, lasers are useful, practical tools. [18]They not used for fighting aliens on Mars, but for helping mankind.

5

Verb Forms
and Their Uses

This chapter will help you avoid or correct mistakes like these:

- Henry hope__ to learn to play a musical instrument.
- He has the idea of enrolled himself in a music school.
- Leslie ___ still taking ballet lessons.
- Both of these schools are offer good education.
- You must to drive carefully.
- I will equipped my car with a pollution-control device.
- Many important things in this world uses electricity.
- Have you ever think what make__ things work?
- My boss told me to turn off the lights, but I forgot to turn off them.
- Everything is depend on me.
- Being humble helps me to get well along with others.

1. English Verb Forms

Refer to the chart below as you go through the following explanation of English verb forms.

English Verb Forms

Timeless Forms			Time-Included Forms		
Base Form	*d-t-n* Form	*-ing* Form	(present) +s Form	(present) No-*s* Form	Past Form
go	gone	going	goes	go	went
eat	eaten	eating	eats	eat	ate
wait	waited	waiting	waits	wait	waited
look	looked	looking	looks	look	looked
break	broken	breaking	breaks	break	broke
put	put	putting	puts	put	put
read	read	reading	reads	read	read
work	worked	working	works	work	worked

1.1 All English verbs have six forms. Three of these forms include (or show) time—either past or present—and three are timeless. Timeless forms do not show time; the aux-words that accompany them do. Time-included forms are not used with aux-words.

Timeless Forms	Time-Included Forms
base form	+*s* form
d-t-n form	no-*s* form
-ing form	past form

1.2 The **base form** of a verb is called the base form because other verb forms are made from it. The base form is the form found in the dictionary. Usually the dictionary shows the other forms of a verb only when they are irregular forms.

1.3 The ***d-t-n* form** is called the *d-t-n* form because it almost always ends in the letter *d, t,* or *n*. (It is sometimes called the **past participle**.) The *d-t-n* form of regular verbs is formed by adding *-ed* to the base form. If the base form ends with the letter *e*, only the *d* is added.

Base Form	*d-t-n* Form
walk	walked
create	created

The *d-t-n* forms of irregular verbs often end in *n* or *t*. Some have different forms.

Base Form	*d-t-n* Form
give	given
leave	left

A few irregular verbs are gradually becoming regular and may have two *d-t-n* forms. Either form is correct.

Base Form	*d-t-n* Forms
dream	dreamt or dreamed
prove	proven or proved

Spelling note: The spelling rules given for the past ending *-ed* in section 1.7 of this chapter apply to the *d-t-n* form also.

1.4 The **-*ing* form** always ends in *-ing*. (It is sometimes called the "**present participle**.") It is usually formed by simply adding *-ing* to the base form. However, there are some exceptions to this rule. Verbs ending with a consonant preceded by any single vowel (except *w*) usually double the final consonant when adding *-ing*.

Base Form	*-ing* Form
hop	hopping
hit	hitting

The final consonant is not doubled if the accent (word stress) falls on the next-to-last syllable of the base form.

Base Form	*-ing* Form
open	opening
develop	developing

Verbs ending in an unpronounced *e* usually drop the *e* before adding *-ing*.

Base Form	*-ing* Form
hope	hoping
write	writing

One-syllable base forms that end in *-ie* substitute *y* for *ie* before the *-ing* is added.

Base Form	*-ing* Form
die	dying

1.5 The **+s form** is called the +s form because it ends in the letter *s*. It is usually formed by adding *s* to the base form. However, there are some exceptions. Base forms that end in the letter *y* preceded by a consonant drop the *y* and add *-ies*.

Base Form	+s Form
try	tries

Base forms that end in the letter *y* preceded by a vowel simply add *-s*.

Base Form	+s Form
play	plays

Base forms that end in *-s, -sh, -ch, -z,* or *-x* add *-es*.

Base Form	+s Form
miss	misses
wish	wishes
catch	catches
buzz	buzzes
fix	fixes

1.6 The **no-*s* form** and the base form look alike. However, although these forms are spelled and pronounced the same way, they are considered separate verb forms because they are used differently. Each form has a distinct function.

1.7 The **past forms** of regular verbs end in *-ed*. If the base form ends with the letter *e*, only the *d* is added.

Base Form	Past Form
finish	finished
complete	completed

Verbs ending in *y* usually change the *y* to *i* and then add *-ed*.

Base Form	Past Form
cry	cried

When the final *y* is preceded by a vowel, it does not change to *i*.

Base Form	Past Form
play	played

Regular verbs ending in a single vowel and consonant often double the final consonant and then add -ed.

Base Form	Past Form
occur	occurred

Some exceptions to this rule are:

1. Verbs of more than one syllable whose base forms are not accented on the last syllable do not double the final consonant.

Base Form	Past Form
remember	remembered

2. Verbs that end in the letter w do not double the w. They add only -ed.

Base Form	Past Form
stew	stewed

Many of the most commonly used verbs have irregular past forms. Appendix C (pages 173–175) lists many of these irregular verbs.

The past form and d-t-n form of some verbs look alike. However, although these forms are spelled and pronounced the same way, they are considered separate verb forms because they are used differently. Each form has a distinct function.

EXERCISE 1-A   *On the chart below, one of the six forms of each of a number of English verbs has been supplied. Complete this chart by writing the other five forms in the appropriate spaces.*

	Timeless Forms			Time-Included Forms		
	Base Form	d-t-n Form	-ing Form	+s Form	No-s Form	Past Form
1.			doing			
2.		gone				
3.	fly					
4.						ate
5.					sleep	
6.	fall					
7.				thinks		
8.		felt				
9.			choosing			
10.						knew

EXERCISE 1-B   *On the chart below, one of the six forms of each of a number of English verbs has been supplied. Complete this chart by writing the other five forms in the appropriate spaces.*

	Timeless Forms			Time-Included Forms		
	Base Form	***d-t-n* Form**	***-ing* Form**	**+*s* Form**	**No-*s* Form**	**Past Form**
1.	rise					
2.			writing			
3.				gives		
4.					become	
5.	keep					
6.		said				
7.						found
8.			losing			
9.				reads		
10.	come					

EXERCISE 1-C   *On the chart below, one of the six forms of each of a number of English verbs has been supplied. Complete this chart by writing the other five forms in the appropriate spaces.*

	Timeless Forms			Time-Included Forms		
	Base Form	***d-t-n* Form**	***-ing* Form**	**+*s* Form**	**No -*s* Form**	**Past Form**
1.				begins		
2.			speaking			
3.					take	
4.	drive					
5.					bring	
6.			buying			
7.		put				
8.						saw
9.	tell					
10.						studied

2. Present Time-Included Forms and Their Uses

In the present tense, there are two time-included verb forms—+*s* and no-*s*. The correct verb form to use depends on the subject of the sentence. This is called subject/verb agreement. (Section 2 of Chapter 4 explained subject/aux-word agreement, a similar concept. Many of the same rules apply to subject/verb agreement.) This explanation is limited to subject/verb agreement. An explanation of the use of time-included forms to indicate different times is given in the next chapter.

2.1   The present tense has two verb forms—the +*s* and the **no-*s***. The +*s* form is used with **singular**, **noncount**, and *-ing* **verb form** subjects (but not with the pronouns *I* and *you*).

> *Doing homework* take**s** time.
> *Richard* always complete**s** his assignments.
> *He* sometimes stay**s** up late to finish them.
> *His dedication* pay**s** off during examinations.

The **no-*s*** form is used with **plural** subjects (and the pronouns *I* and *you*).

> *George and Bill* never complete their homework.
> *They* always stay up late watching television.
> *I* sometimes forget to do my homework.
> *You* hurt yourself when you do your homework carelessly.

2.2   Singular subjects followed by words or phrases such as *as well as, along with, together with, with,* or *like* remain singular (and take +*s* verb forms), although the nouns that follow them may be plural.

> Mary, *along with her friends,* stud**ies** in the library every Saturday.
> The teacher, *together with the students,* work**s** hard.
> Joe, *with his parents,* watch**es** TV every night.

2.3   The expression *one of* is always followed by a **plural** count noun. Because *one* is singular, this expression is followed by the +*s* form of the verb or aux-word.

> *One of* the book**s** ha**s** a page missing.
> *One of* the player**s** seem**s** more enthusiastic than the others.

2.4   The terms *everyone, everybody, everything, no one, nobody, anyone, anybody, anything,* and *none* are **singular**, although they may refer to more than one person. For this reason, they are followed by the +*s* form of the verb or aux-word.

> *Everyone* like**s** Joe.
> *Nobody* hate**s** him.
> *Everybody* like**s** a party.
> *Anybody* know**s** that.
> *No one* ha**s** any money.
> *Everything* take**s** time.

2.5 Noun phrases made with *-ing* verb forms (see Chapter 13, section 5) are singular, even though they sometimes contain plural nouns, and take *+s* verb forms.

> *Jogging* make**s** me tired.
> *Excelling* in sports require**s** dedication.

2.6 Compound subjects (see Chapter 9, section 1) made with *and* are plural and take no-*s* verb forms.

> *Joe and Mark* work in that factory. They both do similar work.
> *Wood, leaves, and paper* burn well if they are dry.

Compound subjects made with *or* may take *+s* or no-*s* verb forms, depending on whether the elements that are compounded are singular or plural.
   If **both elements are singular**, the correct verb form is *+s*.

> *Joe or Mark* work**s** in that factory. (I can't remember which one of them.)

If **both elements are plural**, the correct form is **no-*s***.

> *Seat belts or air bags* protect automobile passengers from injury.

If **one element is singular and the other is plural**, the verb form agrees with the last one (closest to the verb).

> *Mr. Sanchez or his two sons* operate that store. (I can't remember who is
>   in charge now.)
> *The two Sanchez sons or their father* operate**s** that store.

Compound expressions using *either...or...* or its negative counterpart *neither...nor...* follow a similar rule. The verb agrees with the last element.

> *Either Karen Butler or her parents* want to buy that home.
> *Either the Butlers or their daughter Karen* want**s** to buy that home.
>
> *Neither the students nor the teacher* like**s** the classroom.
> *Neither the teacher nor the students* like the classroom.

EXERCISE 2-A   *In each of the blanks write the correct form (+s or no-s) of the verb indicated beneath it. The first one has been done for you.*

SURGERY

[1]Surgery *seems* to be a highly complicated procedure. [2]A surgeon, with
      seem

assistants, _____ well in advance for specialized operations. [3]One
                  plan

of the nurses _____ the instruments. [4]The anesthesiologist, with an
                  supervise

assistant or several assistants, _____ specific duties. [5]Blood pressure
                                      have

_____ monitoring. [6]They _____ respiratory action
      need   watch

and _____ all life signs. [7]Interns or a nurse _____
            check   stand

ready to assist. [8]One of the nurses _____ watching as the surgeon
                                            keep

or the assisting doctors _____ up. [9]This nurse _____
                              scrub   see

that no one _____ to wash his or her hands for the required time
                  fail

and that everyone _____ uncontaminated before the operation
                        remain

_____. [10]Everybody _____ to take the utmost care to
      begin   need

see that everything _____ sterile in the operating room.
                          remain

EXERCISE 2-B   *In each of the blanks write the correct form (+s or no-s) of the verb indicated beneath it. The first one has been done for you.*

ICE

[1]The polar ice pack *presents* a formidable barrier to shipping. [2]In some
                        present

years the ice pack _____ solid, and the Northwest Passage
                        remain

_____ to open as a seagoing lane. [3]Ice breakers _____
      fail   try

in vain to push aside the solid ice. [4]An ice breaker, though strong and powerful,

sometimes _____ frozen in the ice.
                become

[5]In other years when the passage opens, large icebergs _____
                                                                float

southward and _____ shipping in the Atlantic Ocean. [6]A single
                    menace

berg or ice floe _____ thousands of tons and _____
                      weigh   melt

slowly in the frigid water. [7]An iceberg with its huge underwater bulk

_____ against the shore or _____ against other bergs
      jam   grind

with great power.

[8]These icebergs _____ strong boats like matchsticks and
                          crush

_____ hazards at sea. [9]Everyone _____ the story of
       create   know

the *Titanic*, and no one _____ to share that fate.
                                  care

EXERCISE 2-C   *In each of the blanks write the correct form (+s or no-s) of the verb indicated beneath it. The first one has been done for you.*

STARTING A BUSINESS

[1]Richard, with his brothers, *wants* to start his own business. [2]Neither his
                                      want

parents nor his friends _____ he can succeed. [3]Even a small
                                think

business _____ stock and equipment, and of course it also
              need

_____ money to run until it _____ to make a profit.
      require   start

[4]Creditors _____ prompt payment. [5]They _____
                  demand   charge

interest. [6]The government _____ accurate bookkeeping. [7]Even
                                  demand

small businesses _____ countless forms to fill out quarterly.
                       have

[8]Legible reports _____ time to fill out properly. [9]In business,
                         take

time _____ money. [10]Insurance on property and goods
         mean

_____ another financial problem. [11]Richard's father thinks Richard
      pose

and his brothers _____ to forget the idea. [12]Their present jobs
                       need

_____ them an adequate income. [13]His friends _____
      pay   feel

the same way.

3. Past Time-Included Forms and Their Uses

3.1   Every English verb has only one past tense form. It makes no difference whether the subject is singular or plural.

> The *car* crash**ed**.
> The *cars* crash**ed**.
> *He* **went** to town yesterday.
> *They* **went** to town yesterday.

EXERCISE 3-A

Rewrite the paragraph below in the past tense. Add Yesterday *at the beginning of the first sentence and make all the other necessary changes in verb forms. Be sure to eliminate the time expressions that indicate the use of the present tense—usually, frequently, often, and sometimes.*

MARY'S DAY

[1]Mary usually gets up at 6:00 A.M. [2]She takes a shower, gets dressed, and then fixes her breakfast. [3]While she eats breakfast, she listens to the morning news broadcast. [4]Mary rides to work on the bus and arrives at the office about eight o'clock. [5]She frequently works without a break until 11:30. [6]Then she takes an hour for lunch. [7]She eats a sandwich that she takes with her so she has time to go shopping. [8]Mary returns to the office at 12:30 and works until four o'clock. [9]However, she takes a half-hour break at two o'clock. [10]Mary takes the bus home again but often stops for dinner at a small restaurant near her home. [11]She sometimes has a date for the evening and gets home tired but happy around midnight.

EXERCISE 3-B

Rewrite the paragraph below in the past tense. Change Here stands *to* There stood *and make all the other necessary changes in verb forms.*

MAKING A MOVIE

[1]Here stands a Hollywood movie set. [2]Cameras grind away as the action begins. [3]Heroes, heroines, and villains share the spotlight. [4]Each tries to capture the limelight. [5]None of them really succeeds. [6]Painted backdrops and a false-fronted house serve as a background for the scenes. [7]A stunt man leaps into action as the star hides in the shadows ready to stand at the side of the recently rescued heroine. [8]The villain and the hero trade punches which fall short of their mark, although the men stagger and fall as though struck. [9]The film records the action as each actor or actress acts passionately for the faithful moviegoers who enjoy the vicarious thrills of another Western.

EXERCISE 3-C

Rewrite the paragraph below in the past tense. Add When I was young, *to the beginning of the first sentence. Make all the other necessary changes in verb forms.*

FADS AND FASHIONS

[1]Fads and fashions come and go. [2]Men's and women's clothes change with the season and the year. [3]People dress for fashion rather than comfort. [4]When it is stylish, feet crowd into narrow, pointed shoes. [5]Hard, inflexible wooden slabs become fashionable and replace soft leather shoes, not on country lanes and cobblestone roads but on city streets and hardwood floors.

[6]Fashion dictates the food people eat as well. [7]One year, refined foods replace natural foods. [8]The next, cooked foods supplant raw ones. [9]Fads and fashions support change. [10]New things replace old ones. [11]Then the cycle starts again.

EXERCISE 3.1-A

Rewrite the following paragraph in the past tense. Change the first sentence to I once had a perfect class. *When necessary, change the verbs and the aux-words in the other sentences to past forms.*

A TEACHER'S DREAM

[1]I have a perfect class. [2]I love my professional life. [3]I can scarcely wait to get to my classroom. [4]The students all come to class early. [5]They have written all their homework carefully and neatly. [6]They are prepared for the day's work. [7]Everyone listens intently as I give the lecture. [8]No one whispers or is inattentive. [9]The

questions that are asked are intelligent and thought-provoking. ¹⁰I always know the answers and the students are delighted to learn more about the subject. ¹¹The students hate to leave so they linger after class is over because they want to know more. ¹²Between classes they diligently go to the library to do research on the subjects we are studying. ¹³The students and I look forward to the discussions we will have during the next class period. ¹⁴Turning in grades becomes an easy task with such students who study for knowledge and care very little about report cards.

EXERCISE 3.1-B   *Rewrite the following paragraph in the past tense. Put* Last year, *at the beginning of the first sentence. When necessary, change the verbs and aux-words in the other sentences to past forms.*

A PROFESSIONAL GOLFER

¹John Jones plays golf to make money. ²He is a professional golfer. ³This seems like an easy and pleasant life. ⁴However, this is not the case. ⁵He is away from his family most of the year. ⁶If he drops out of the professional tour he can't make a living. ⁷Even then, unless he has a sponsor, in a bad year his living depends on his earlier winnings which he has saved. ⁸Constant practice is necessary as he has to stay in top physical condition. ⁹His competition never lets up. ¹⁰One bad stroke can put him out of the money. ¹¹The crowd, which follows the golfers around the course, constantly praises or boos him. ¹²Jones, along with his caddy, ignores the crowd if he expects to finish in the money. ¹³Although golfer Jones's winnings may be high or low, expenses remain fixed. ¹⁴Professional fees have to be paid before he enters a tournament. ¹⁵It costs him a lot of money to travel, as the tournaments are held in different sections of the United States and many occur in other countries. ¹⁶Hotel and food bills take a sizable sum. ¹⁷Added to this is the cost of expensive equipment—clubs, balls, etc. ¹⁸John Jones, like many other pros, plays professional golf to establish a name so he can quit, stay home, and really make money advertising sports equipment on TV.

EXERCISE 3.1-C   *Rewrite the following paragraph in the past tense. Change the first sentence to* When I saw him last year, Roger had a new job. *When necessary, change the verbs and aux-words in the other sentences to past forms.*

A NEW JOB

¹Roger has a new job. ²He is very happy with it. ³He can come and go as he pleases. ⁴He drives a company car to and from work. ⁵He meets many interesting people as he travels throughout the country. ⁶His company pays his hotel and food bills when he is away from home. ⁷Above all, the pay is good. ⁸He is thinking of taking a correspondence course so he can learn more about business procedures and bookkeeping. ⁹Possibly this will lead to an even better position. ¹⁰There are lots of possibilities for advancement in his company.

4. Timeless Verb Forms and Their Uses

Refer to the following chart as you go through the explanation (below the chart) of how English verb forms are used. This explanation is limited to aux-word/verb combinations and agreement between subjects and aux-words. An explanation of the use of aux-words and verbs in relation to time is given in Chapter 6.

English Verb Forms

Timeless Forms			Time-Included Forms		
Base Form	***d-t-n* Form**	***-ing* Form**	**(Present) + s Form**	**(Present) No-s Form**	**Past Form**
go	gone	going	goes	go	went
eat	eaten	eating	eats	eat	ate
wait	waited	waiting	waits	wait	waited
look	looked	looking	looks	look	looked
break	broken	breaking	breaks	break	broke
put	put	putting	puts	put	put
read	read	reading	reads	read	read
work	worked	working	works	work	worked

Present	**Past**	**Present**	**Past**	**Present**	**Past**	*(does)*	*(do)*	*(did)*

Hidden Aux-Words

will	*would*	*have*	*had*	*is/am*	*was*
can	*could*	*has*		*are*	*were*
do/does	*did*				
shall	*should*	**base**	***-ing***	**base**	***d-t-n***	***-ing***
may	*might*					
must		*have*	*having*	*be*	*been*	*being*

Aux-Words

4.1 The verb form used with an aux-word must be one of the three timeless forms (*base*, *d-t-n*, or *-ing*). These verb forms do not indicate time; the aux-word does. When used as verbs, all timeless verb forms are preceded by an aux-word.

4.2 The **base form** of a verb usually follows a **modal** or a **"hidden" aux-word** (made "visible" to form a question, etc.).

Aux-Word	**Base Form**
I	go.
He will	work.
She doesn't	care.

When the function word *to* precedes the base form, the resulting combination (often called the **infinitive**) is used as a noun. This is explained in Chapter 13, section 5.

The **base form** is also used following other verbs such as *have to* and *used to* and in most other places where a verb form follows *to*.

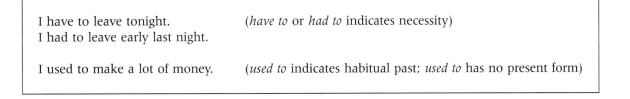

I have to leave tonight.   (*have to* or *had to* indicates necessity)
I had to leave early last night.

I used to make a lot of money.   (*used to* indicates habitual past; *used to* has no present form)

After some special verb expressions ending in *to*, however, other verb forms are used (see section 4.4).

The **base form** follows the object of certain verbs, such as *let, make,* and *hear.* In this case, the base form indicates the action of the object. (See Chapter 7, section 10.2).

My father won't *let* me *go.*
She *made* my brother *work.*
I have *heard* her *tell* that story many times.

4.3 The *d-t-n* **form**, in a basic sentence, is used after the aux-words which are forms of *have.*

Aux-Word	d-t-n Form
They have	gone.
He has	worked.

In the passive transformation (explained in Chapter 10) the *d-t-n* form follows a form of the aux-word *be.*

My uncle was attacked by two lions.

The *d-t-n* form may also be used as a **modifier** (explained in Chapters 8 and 11). In this case it does not function as a verb and needs no aux-word.

The shrunken head shocked the explorers.

4.4 The *-ing* **form**, when used as a verb, follows the aux-words which are forms of *be* (i.e., *is, am, are, was, were, be,* and *been*).

Aux-Word		-*ing* Form
I	am	going.
He	is	working.

The *-ing* form is also used after prepositions.

By working hard, she earned a fortune.
After returning home, he took off his shoes.

The *-ing* form is also used after certain verb expressions ending in *to.*

I am *looking forward to* meeting you.
He was not *accustomed to* sitting on the floor.
They *devote* their time *to* buying and selling.

The *-ing* form follows the objects of certain verbs, such as *hear, see,* etc. In this case, the *-ing* form indicates that the action of the object is repeated or in progress over a period of time (see Chapter 7, section 10.2).

> I heard the window *banging* in the wind.
> I saw him *running* across the field.
> In my mind, I can still hear her *singing*.

When the *-ing* form is used as a **modifier** (explained in Chapters 8, section 5 and Chapter 11), it does not need to be preceded by an aux-word.

> *Flowering* trees usually bloom in the spring.

When the *-ing* form is used to begin a **noun phrase** (explained in Chapter 13, section 5; traditionally called a **gerund**), it may be used as a subject, object, etc., and does not need to be preceded by an aux-word.

> *Swimming* is good exercise.
> *Studying* all night leaves me unable to think clearly the next day.
> I hate *jogging*.

4.5 The three time-included verb forms (+*s*, no-*s*, and past) contain the **hidden aux-words** *does, do,* and *did*. When these hidden aux-words are taken out and used to form negatives, to form yes/no questions, or for emphasis, the time-included forms change to the timeless base form of the verb. (This was explained in Chapter 4.)

	He		**likes** detective stories. +*s*	(statement)
Does aux	he		**like** detective stories? base	(yes/no question)
	He		**doesn't** **like** detective stories. aux base	(negative statement)
	His parents		**like** detective stories. no-*s*	(statement)
Do aux	his parents		**like** detective stories? base	(yes/no question)
	His parents		**don't** **like** detective stories. aux base	(negative statement)

4.6 The chart below summarizes the main points of aux-word/verb agreement:

Aux-Word or Preposition →	Form of Verb or Aux-Word
none (hidden)	time-included (+s, no-s, past)
modal	base
do, does, did	
to	
have, has, had	d-t-n
be (passive)	
be	-ing
preposition	

EXERCISE 4-A

Supply the correct timeless form (base, d-t-n, or -ing) of the verb or aux-word indicated beneath each blank.

TONGUE TWISTERS

¹Repetitive sounds have _____ the basis for riddles, puns, and
    form

tongue twisters in all languages. ²They must _____ said aloud or
    be

they can't _____ fully appreciated. ³If one repeats any combination
    be

of sounds often enough and fast enough, the sounds will _____
    become

strange sounding or distorted. ⁴Two similar sounds that have _____
    be

placed together are often confused. ⁵Probably the sibilants, or hissing sounds, in

English have _____ the majority of tongue twisters, although "Peter
    produce

Piper and his pickled peppers" has always _____ popular. ⁶Children
    be

have _____ fun with the relatively easy "She sells seashells by the
    have

seashore," while adults will usually _____ the more sophisticated
    try

"The sixth sick sheik's sixth sheep's sick." ⁷You might _____ to find
    like

a book and try a few English tongue twisters. ⁸You should _____
    plan

on lots of practice. ⁹After you have _____ a lot of time and can
    spend

_____ them easily and perfectly, you might _____ your
    repeat   *impress*

friends with your linguistic ability.

EXERCISE 4-B   *Supply the correct timeless form (base, d-t-n, or -ing) of the verb or aux-word indicated beneath each blank.*

EARTHQUAKES

¹A recent earthquake has _____ the lives of over twenty
                                    take

thousand people. ²It has _____ thousands more without homes and
                                leave

family. ³Although scientists have _____ earthquake-prone places,
                                        locate

anywhere in the world the earth could _____ to shake at any
                                            start

moment. ⁴The tremor might _____ or _____ to shake
                                subside   continue

until buildings have _____ and people have _____
                        topple   be

killed and hurt.

⁵Earthquakes have long _____ one of nature's most curious
                            be

phenomena. ⁶So far, only astrologers or other pseudo-scientists have

_____ to _____ the specific location or time
    attempt   predict

of an earthquake. ⁷However, scientists are _____ to find a
                                                try

way to _____ earthquakes. ⁸They are _____ the
            predict   measure

slightest bulge in the earth's surface in earthquake-prone places. ⁹They

have _____ and _____ many of the faults where
        chart   name

buckling has _____. ¹⁰Hopefully, before too long scientists
                occur

will _____ to predict tremors so people can leave these places
        learn

temporarily and avoid much death and suffering.

EXERCISE 4-C   *Supply the correct timeless form (base, d-t-n, or -ing) of the verb or aux-word indicated beneath each blank. Remember, the -ing form follows prepositions.*

READ THE LABEL

¹Many people have never _____ or _____ to
                                learn   bother

_____ the labels on the packages or cans of food they buy
    read

daily. ²By just _____ at the pictures on a container one doesn't
                    look

_____ very much about the product. ³By law, all packaged
    learn

food must _____ the contents of the container. ⁴This list
                list

will _____ the preservatives as well as the main ingredients.
            include

[5]People can _____ illness by _____ if anything
                  prevent   see

they have _____ that they are allergic to is included. [6]They can
              find

_____ malnutrition by _____ preparations to which
      avoid   select

essential vitamins and minerals have _____ added. [7]One should
                                              be

_____ the order of the ingredients on the label since it indicates
      notice

the relative amount of each ingredient. [8]The most common ingredient must

_____ first on the list. [9]A consumer should _____
      appear   become

knowledgeable about labels. [10]One can _____ money and
                                              save

_____ better health by _____ them carefully.
      have   examine

5. Multiple Aux-Word/Verb Combinations

More than one aux-word can be used at a time. When this is done, only the first aux-word shows time. The aux-words which follow must be timeless forms.

Modals do **not** have timeless forms. Therefore, only one of them can be used in an aux-word/verb group and it must come first in the group.

The other aux-words (*have, has, had, is, am, are, was,* and *were*) have **timeless** forms as follows:

Base	d-t-n	-ing
be have	been	being (having)

These timeless aux-words function the same way and in the same order that timeless verb forms do:

the **base** forms *have* and *be* follow the modals (or their negative forms) and *to*

the **d-t-n** form *been* follows any form of *have* (and forms of *be* in passive transformations [Chapter 10])

the **-ing** form *being* follows any form of *be* and prepositions

the **-ing** form *having* is used only when making half sentences (explained in Chapter 11).

Subject	Modal	*have*	*be*		Remainder of sentence
He	could	**have** base	**been** *d-t-n*		in the accident.
He			is	**being** *-ing*	funny.
He	will		**be** base		leaving soon.

6. Phrasal Verbs

6.1 A phrasal verb looks like a verb followed by a preposition (or two prepositions), but it is very different in use and meaning.

The second (and sometimes third) word of a phrasal verb is called the *particle*. Unlike a preposition, which always shows location or direction, the particle may add emphasis, show completion, or result in an entirely new and different meaning.

EXAMPLE:

Susan *opened up* a new store. (emphasis)
Ted *chopped down* the tree. (completion)
Gale *turned on* the television. (new meaning: compare the pictures below)

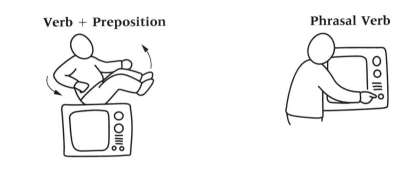

Verb + Preposition   **Phrasal Verb**

6.2 It is sometimes important to distinguish between a phrasal verb and a verb followed by a preposition, but it is not always easy. For making this distinction, the following four tests are useful (if one doesn't help, try another).

TEST 1.   Divide the sentence in half between the verb and the preposition or particle. Then move the second part to the front of the sentence.

If the meaning of the sentence remains the same, then what you have divided is a verb and a preposition.

If this process renders the sentence meaningless, ridiculous, or otherwise unacceptable, or changes the meaning, you are dealing with a phrasal verb.

> George **ran** / **up** a large hill.
> **Up** a large hill George **ran**. (Acceptable. This is a verb + preposition.)
>
> George **ran** / **up** a large bill. (He had a lot of debts to pay.)
> **Up** a large bill George **ran**. (Not acceptable. This is a phrasal verb.)

TEST 2.   Remove the preposition or particle (and any phrase which follows).

If the meaning of the verb remains the same (even though some additional meaning may have been lost), then the deleted word is probably a preposition.

If the deleted word is the particle of a phrasal verb, then the meaning of the verb will usually change significantly.

> Harry **looked over** the car and saw George on the sidewalk.
> Harry **looked** . . . and saw George on the sidewalk.
>   (Same meaning = verb + preposition)

> Harry **looked over** (examined) the car and decided to buy it.
> Harry **looked** . . . and decided to buy it.
>   (Different meaning = phrasal verb)

TEST 3. Often a single-word verb can be substituted for a phrasal verb without changing the meaning. (Notice that this substitution often raises the level of formality.) There is a list of such substitutes in Appendix D (page 176).
  This substitution cannot be done with a normal verb and preposition.

> Alex **looked over** the used car. (phrasal verb)
> Alex **examined** the used car. (single-word substitution)
> Alex **looked over** the fence at his neighbor's lawn. (verb + preposition)
>   (There is no single-word substitute for *look over* in this sentence.)

TEST 4. Frequently the prepositional phrase following a verb answers the question "Where?" This is not usually the case with a phrasal verb particle although some particles do show location or direction.

> Brenda **ran across** the bridge to escape. (verb + preposition)
>   Q: Where did Brenda run to escape?
>   A: Across the bridge.
> Brenda **ran across** the missing book in her desk drawer. (phrasal verb)
>   Q: Where did Brenda run in her desk drawer?
>   (Since it is made from a sentence with a phrasal verb, this question is inappropriate, and there is no acceptable answer.)

6.3 Some two-word phrasal verbs become three-word phrasal verbs by adding a second particle. This is possible only when there is an object.

> Joe **got out** (i.e., Joe escaped.). (two-word phrasal verb)
> Joe **got out of** the difficult situation. (three-word phrasal verb)

EXERCISE 6-A *In the story below, the verbs followed by particles (phrasal verbs) or prepositions have been italicized. Circle only the phrasal verbs.*

JOHN'S CAR

[1]The minute John *got up* this morning, he *ran out* to the garage behind his house. [2]He *opened up* his toolbox and began to *work on* his car. [3]He was trying to *figure out* why his car wouldn't *start up*. [4]He *looked at* everything, but he couldn't *pin down* the reason. [5]He *filled up* the gas tank, *checked under* the hood, *tuned up* the engine,

hooked up a loose wire, and even *took apart* the carburetor. [6]He tried everything he could *think of*, but the car still wouldn't *start up*. [7]He finally *gave up*.

[8]*To take* his mind *off* the car, John *went in* the house, *sat down on* the couch, and *turned on* the television. [9]That didn't *help* him *out*, though. [10]A do-it-yourself auto-mechanic program was on. [11]He *watched* it *for* a few minutes until he *came up with* an idea of what might be wrong with his car. [12]Then he *went out* and started *working on* it again.

EXERCISE 6-B

In the story below, the verbs followed by particles (phrasal verbs) or prepositions have been italicized. Circle only the phrasal verbs.

A FRIEND IN NEED

[1]The other morning, just after I *woke up*, my friend Harry *called* me *up* and asked me to *hurry over* to his place. [2]It seemed that he and his girlfriend had *broken up* the night before, and he was feeling really sad.

[3]Well, I *hurried up* and *gobbled down* my breakfast and *ran out* of the house. [4]I *hopped in* my old car and turned the key, but nothing happened. [5]It wouldn't even *turn over*. [6]I had *left* the lights *on* overnight, and the battery had *run down*. [7]It was completely dead.

[8]Nevertheless, a friend in need is a friend indeed, so I *jumped on* my brother's motorcycle and *started over* to Harry's house. [9]Our neighbor's dog, which hates me, saw its chance and *ran out* furiously. [10]*Chasing after* me, with one big bite it *took* a big piece *out* of my pants. [11]However, that didn't stop me, and I *continued on*. [12]A few blocks down the road I *ran out* of gas. [13]I *jumped off* and *ran to* the corner gas station. [14]I had to *put* the gas *in* a can and then *run back* to the motorcycle. [15]Finally, I *pulled up* in front of Harry's house.

[16]I *hopped off* the motorcycle and *ran up* to the front door and *knocked on* it. [17]Harry's mother *came out* and said, "Oh, Harry isn't here." [18]Just after I had *hung up* the phone, he had *called* his girlfriend *up*. [19]They had *made up* over the phone and Harry had *gone over* to see her.

EXERCISE 6-C

In the story below, the verbs followed by particles (phrasal verbs) or prepositions have been italicized. Circle only the phrasal verbs.

AN ORDERLY CLASSROOM

[1]In an orderly classroom everything works smoothly. [2]When the students *come into* the classroom they *hand in* their homework. [3]The students' notebooks are organized so they don't have to waste time *looking for* their homework assignments. [4]They *sit* quietly *at* their desks. [5]The teacher *hands out* their papers which have been corrected. [6]When the teacher tells the students to *open up* their books, they *turn to* the right page and *look over* the lesson together. [7]The students don't whisper and *talk to* each other. [8]No one has to *wake up* sleeping students. [9]There are no inattentive or lazy students who *fall behind* and have to *catch up* later.

[10]As the teacher talks, the students *take down* orderly notes so that if they have a question later they can *look up* the answer and find it. [11]As students *think of* questions, they ask the teacher. [12]No one speaks without *putting up* his hand and *waiting for* the teacher to *call on* him.

[13]At the end of the class period, the teacher *hands out* the assignment for the next day and the students *stand up* and *go out* the door. [14]The teacher *picks up* any papers that have been *dropped on* the floor or any books that have been *left behind*, erases the blackboard, and *turns off* the lights before leaving.

7. Separable and Inseparable Phrasal Verbs

7.1   There are two kinds of phrasal verbs, **separable** and **inseparable**. The phrasal verbs included in Appendix D (page 176) are divided into these two categories.

7.2   An object cannot be placed between the verb and the particle of an **inseparable** phrasal verb.

The teacher **called on** the students.
The teacher **called** the students **on**. (unacceptable)

My mother **looked for** my brother.
My mother **looked** my brother **for**. (unacceptable)

(An object cannot be placed between a verb and *preposition* either.)

7.3   An object **may** be placed between the verb and the particle of a **separable** phrasal verb. It may also occur after the particle. Either position is acceptable.

Susan **called up** John.
Susan **called** John **up**. (both acceptable)

Mr. Garcia **filled out** the form.
Mr. Garcia **filled** the form **out**. (both acceptable)

7.4   When the object of a **separable** phrasal verb is a **pronoun**, it must be placed **between** the verb and the particle.

The pilot **tried out** the new airplane.
The pilot **tried** it **out**. (acceptable)
The pilot **tried** out it. (unacceptable)

EXERCISE 7-A   *Answer the following questions in the affirmative or negative, using complete sentences (long answers). In your answers, use appropriate pronouns in place of the objects (in boldface). The first two have been done for you.*

STUDYING

1. Did you go over **your in-class notes after class yesterday**?

   Yes, I went over them.

2. Did you mix up **the assignments made by the teacher**?

   No, I didn't mix them up.

3. Did you try to get out of **doing your homework**?

4. Did you put off **doing your homework last night**?

5. Did you finally get around to **doing your homework**?

6. Did you get through with **your homework** before midnight?

7. Did you look up **the unfamiliar words** in the dictionary?

8. Did you show up for **class** on time today?

9. Did you hand in **your homework** when the teacher asked for it?

10. Did you think of **the right answers to the teacher's questions**?

11. Did you use up **all your notebook paper** writing an in-class essay?

12. Did you leave out **the important punctuation marks**?

13. Did you go over **your essay** to check it for mistakes?

14. Did you do over **the parts that were wrong**?

15. Did you talk over **your problems** with your teacher?

EXERCISE 7-B   *Answer the following questions in the affirmative or negative, using complete sentences (long answers). In your answers, use appropriate pronouns in place of the objects (in boldface).*

TODAY'S ACTIVITIES

1. Did your alarm clock wake **you** up early this morning?

2. Did you make up **your daily to-do list**?

3. Did you keep up with **your schedule**?

4. Did you wait for **help from someone else?**

5. Did you dive into **your work** alone?

6. Did you clean up **your room**?

7. Did you take out **the trash**?

8. Did you put away **your things**?

9. Did you pick up **the mail**?

10. Did you look for **ways to make your work more pleasant**?

11. Did you get through with **what you planned to do**?

12. Did you have to put off **your last few tasks** until tomorrow?

13. Did you run out of **energy** by the end of the day?

14. Did you make up **your mind** to do things differently tomorrow?

15. Did you turn off **all the lights** before going to bed?

EXERCISE 7-C   *Answer the following questions in the affirmative or negative, using complete sentences (long answers). In your answers, use appropriate pronouns in place of the objects (in boldface).*

HARRY'S TROUBLED LIFE

1. Did Harry get into **trouble** early in life?

2. Did he fool around in **school**?

3. Did he fall behind **his classmates**?

4. Did he get into **fights** often?

5. Did he drop out of **school** as soon as he could?

6. Did he fall in with **bad company**?

7. Did he pick up **bad habits and ideas** from his new friends?

8. Did he take part in **a number of robberies**?

9. Did he later hold up **a bank**?

10. Did he blow open **the safe**?

11. Did he get away with **robbery** the first few times?

12. Did the law finally catch up with **Harry**?

13. Did he finally wake up?

14. Did he make up **his mind** to go straight?

15. Did he clean up **his life**?

8. Proofreading

As explained previously, an important part of the process of writing is proofreading. Although you now have a better understanding of English verb forms and how they are used, you may still make occasional mistakes with them.

The following exercises will give you practice in focused proofreading. The passages contain numerous mistakes with verb forms, but that is the only type of error they contain. Using what you have learned in this chapter, focus on finding and fixing the incorrect verb forms.

EXERCISE 8-A

In the paragraphs below, there are a number of errors involving verb forms (wrong form, misspelling, lack of agreement with subject, incorrectly divided phrasal verb, etc.). Find the errors, correct them, and then rewrite the passage. Do not add, remove, or change any words except verb forms.

ORIGAMI—PART I

[1]Origami is the Japanese art of paper folding. [2]Since the fourteenth century, people in Japan have been created likenesses of birds, fish, and frogs from flat sheets of paper. [3]Traditionally, origami artists have make models of living creatures. [4]Of course, using origami techniques, it is possible to producing models of many other things. [5]Some present-day experts, for example, have create models of modern objects, such as jet planes.

[6]By tradition, origami artists must made models only by fold the paper. [7]They cannot cutting it. [8]Nevertheless, they can still produce an amazing variety of creations. [9]One famous Japanese artist can even turns a square piece of paper into a self-portrait of his own face.

[10]People who do not knew about origami are usually amazed at the results. [11]They think it must be very difficult to fold paper into such intricate models. [12]Of course, some complex models are very difficult, but others are quite easy to make and requires only a few folds.

EXERCISE 8-B   *In the paragraphs below, there are a number of errors involving verb forms (wrong form, misspelling, lack of agreement with subject, incorrectly divided phrasal verb, etc.). Find the errors, correct them, and then rewrite the passage. Do not add, remove, or change any words except verb forms.*

ORIGAMI—PART II

[1]Origami can be frustrating. [2]In the process of make a model, you must followed instructions carefully. [3]If you don't carry out each step precisely and in proper sequence, the result will not look like what you started out to make. [4]You may not even produce a final product at all.

[5]On the other hand, origami can also be therapeutic. [6]It can provides a healthy distraction for the sick. [7]A hospital worker once interested a girl in try to folding a bird. [8]The girl had not spoke a word for years. [9]Nevertheless, the next day, she runs to the nurse with a paper bird in her hand. [10]She was shouted, "I made it! I made it!" [11]The girl was so excited that she did not noticed that she was speak.

[12]You don't have to be Japanese to learning origami. [13]There are many English-language books on origami that provides step-by-step instructions for making models. [14]All you have to do is go to a bookstore that carrys origami books, pick one out, and buy it. [15]Some comes complete with colored paper squares to fold. [16]You may also found a book about origami in your school library. [17]If so, check out it, taking it home, and try make a simple model. [18]You just might discovers a lifelong hobby that will brings you much pleasure.

EXERCISE 8-C   *In the paragraphs below, there are a number of errors involving verb forms (wrong form, misspelling, lack of agreement with subject, incorrectly divided phrasal verb, etc.). Find the errors, correct them, and then rewrite the passage. Do not add, remove, or change any words except verb forms.*

A STRANGE ORCHESTRA

[1]On a warm summer day or evening, you can often hears the music of the strangest musicians on earth. [2]I am not refer to human beings but to insects. [3]Grasshoppers and cicadas, for example, made music in some very strange ways.

[4]The grasshopper play its own type of violin. [5]It stands on its four front "hands" and use its thighbone as a bow. [6]It rubbing this "bow" on a row of small, stiff bumps on its wing. [7]This action produced a rapid clicking sound. [8]You have probably hear it if you have walking across a meadow in the summer.

[9]Cicadas making music in a very different way. [10]They has special sound organs on the sides of their bodies under special plates beneath their wings. [11]These organs looks like small pits, and inside of them there are tiny "drumheads." [12]When a cicada wants to making its mating call, it open the plates that cover the pits. [13]At the same time, special muscles pull the drumheads and makes them vibrate. [14]The pits amplifys the sound into the shrill, piercing noise you may have hear on a hot afternoon.

[15]Other insects, making noises in equally unusual ways. [16]Some beetles clicks. [17]Crickets chirping by rub parts of their wings together. [18]Flies, bees, and mosquitoes makes sounds by vibrate their wings thousands of times a minute. [19]When you puts all these insect "musicians" together, they truly made a fascinating orchestra.

6

Verbs and Time

This chapter will help you avoid or correct mistakes like these:

- Sally does not have a steady boyfriend, but she <u>had</u> a lot of good friends.
- Allen <u>move</u> to London in 1985.
- Before people discovered electricity, we <u>have</u> to use candles and lamps for light.
- I <u>live</u> in this town since 1972.
- Your flowers <u>are smelling</u> very beautiful.
- Those students <u>have started</u> school here five years ago.
- Mr. Randall told me he <u>will</u> return in a few minutes.
- I <u>start</u> this course last year.
- Without electricity, we <u>will</u> still use candles for light.

1. Time and Tense

1.1   *Time* and *tense* are not synonyms—that is, they do not mean the same thing. **Time** is what we measure with clocks and calendars. We usually think of it in terms of past, present, and future. It is the same throughout the world. **Tense** is the inflection or changing of an aux-word or verb form. In English, these changes usually occur at the end of the word. Tenses (and aspects of tenses) are used to show time, time relationships, real/unreal conditions, and aspects such as completion or continuation of an action. The rules for tense formation and use are different in every language.

1.2   In English we can write about many different times, but we use only two tenses—present or past. Each of these tenses has various aspects (to be explained in this chapter).

Remember that English verbs (and most aux-words) have both time-included and timeless forms. There are three time-included forms—two present and one past. The other forms are timeless. (This was explained in Chapter 5.)

In English the various time relationships, conditions, and aspects mentioned above (in section 1.1) are shown with various combinations of these verb forms, aux-words, and time expressions.

1.3   Each language has its own way of looking at time and expressing time relationships. Trying to translate or transfer the time categories from one language to another one (i.e., from your native language to English) can lead to serious errors. Instead, when you learn a new language and its tenses you must also learn to think about time in a new way.

2. Establishing and Changing Time

2.1   In formal writing, it is customary to establish a particular time—past or present. Time is established by...

1. **a time expression**

> Yesterday...(past time)
> Every day...(present time)

and/or
2. **the tense of the aux-word or verb form itself.**

> John goes...(present tense = present time)
> John went...(past tense = past time)

(Important: The aux-word or verb tense must agree with the time indicated by the time expression.)

2.2   Once a time is established, it should **not** be changed **without**...

1. **a signal** (a time expression)

> **Yesterday**, I **had** many things to do, but **today** I **have** a lot of
> (past time   (past   (present   (present
>   signal)   tense)   time   tense)
>   signal)
>
> free time.

and

2. **a valid reason.**

> When we **saw** the sunrise, we **knew** we **were** facing east because the
>   (past)   (past)   (past)
>
> sun **always comes** up in the east. (Reason for changing: general truth)
>   (present (present
>   time   tense)
>   signal)

2.3   One way of understanding this rule is to compare it with driving on a multilane highway.

A poor (and dangerous) driver switches lanes frequently for no reason at all and does not give the proper turn signal. (An even more dangerous driver signals one direction and then turns the other way.)

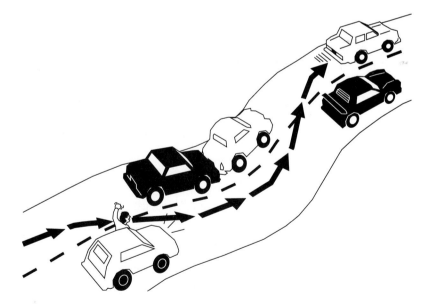

A good driver changes lanes only when necessary and only after giving the proper turn signal.

In the same way, a good writer changes tenses (e.g., past to present, or present to past) only when such a change is necessary and appropriate. When the change is made, a clear signal is provided in the form of a time expression, new paragraph, etc.

2.4   It is possible and permissible, however, to switch to a **later or earlier time** within the **same tense** (present or past) without using a time expression. This is done—without switching tenses—by using aux-words.

> Anna **promised** that she **would write** me a letter.
> (past tense)   (later time in the past)
>
> Charlie **claims** that he **has caught** more fish than I **have**.
> (present tense)   (earlier time in the present)

Later sections of this chapter explain how this is done.

3. The Simple Present Tense and Time

3.1   The simple present tense is used for things that happen "all the time." A more formal way of saying this is **customary or habitual action**.

Time expressions often used with customary action include *annually, always, every day, usually, rarely, often, frequently, occasionally, sometimes, never, once in a while,* etc.

> I often go to town.
> John rarely comes to see me.
> He usually attends the meetings.
> He frequently swims at four o'clock.
> He jogs every morning.

3.2   The simple present tense is also used to express **general truths**.

> The administration sets the fees.
> The planets revolve around the sun.
> Water freezes at zero degrees Centigrade.
> The moon circles around the Earth.

3.3   The simple present tense is also used to express **ability**, even if the action is in progress at the present moment.

> She swims very well.
> I teach music.
> Mary plays the piano, but John plays the trombone.

3.4   In addition, the simple present tense is used with "nonprogressive" verbs such as *see, hope, hear, smell, feel, seem, look, want, remember, forget, prefer, appear, know, imagine, own,* etc., which express **perception, possession, mental or emotional states or conditions,** and **measurement** even if the meaning refers only to the immediate present and not "all the time."

I have a headache.
He seems distressed.
I need some information.
I want something to eat.
I remember the facts now.
The cheese smells bad.
The hamburger tastes delicious.
I know the answer to your question.
This package weighs ten pounds.

3.5   When certain verbs are used with future time expressions, **future time** (for planned, scheduled events) may be expressed in the simple present tense.

Some future time expressions are *tomorrow, next week, next summer, Monday, Tuesday, in January, in February, at eight o'clock, before six o'clock,* etc.

We leave tomorrow.
The train arrives at ten tonight.
James starts his trip next week.
Mary gets home in the morning.

4. The Simple Past Tense and Time

4.1   The simple past tense is used to write about things that existed or occurred at a **definite** or **specific** time in the past. This definite, specific time is often indicated by time expressions such as *yesterday, last week, ten years ago,* etc.

She went home an hour ago.
I received a package from home yesterday.
Our team won the game Saturday night.
Mary played the piano while Jane sang.

Note: When the simple past tense is used, it is usually possible to specify a definite time when answering a *when* question about the statement.

Q: When did she go home?
A: An hour ago.

Q: When did our team win the game?
A: Saturday night.

In the course of a paragraph or story, the past time may move from one definite past time to another definite past time.

In my youth I lived in a small town. Later, we moved to the big city. After several years, my father bought a farm and we moved to a rural area.

4.2   The simple past tense may also be used to write about activities that existed or occurred:

1. **over a period of time** in the past, or

> They played for several hours.
> He played rugby while he was in college.
> I waited for her all afternoon.
> During the semester break, the students went home.

2. **at intervals** in the past (**customary** or **habitual**).

> She usually arrived late to the meetings last semester.
> He visited his mother from time to time.
> She walked to school every day when he was young.
> I heard the chimes regularly last year.

Another way of showing customary activity in the past is by using *used to*. (*Used to* has only a *past* and a *base* form) or the modal *would* (see Chapter 4, section 8.2).

> I used to go to school every day.
> Did you use to get there on time?
> When I was young, I would swim every day during summer vacation.

4.3   When writing about something which is **hypothetical, imaginary,** or **unreal,** it is common to use **past** tense even though the imagining is going on in the **present**. Section 11 of this chapter explains how and when this is done.

> If I were the president, I would eliminate taxes; however, I am not, so I must pay them.

EXERCISE 4-A   *Supply the correct* present *or* past *form of the verb or aux-word whose base form is beneath the blank.*

FRESH BREAD

¹Whenever I _____ fresh bread baking, I _____ of my
                        smell   think

youth and what fun it _____ when I _____ home from
                              be   come

school and _____ fresh loaves of bread on the table. ²Even now, if
                  find

I _____ my eyes, I _____ to taste the goodness of a thick
        close   seem

slab of that bread lavishly spread with butter. ³Our family _____
                                                                      seem

to eat the bread as fast as Mother _____ make it. ⁴Twice a week she
                                          can

_____ a new batch. ⁵I always _____ all I _____,
      bake   eat   can

yet I never _____ of that good bread my mother _____.
                      tire   bake

⁶Bread _____ truly the "staff of life."
         be

EXERCISE 4-B

Supply the correct present _or_ past _form of the verb or aux-word whose base form is beneath the blank._

TASTE

¹Food frequently _____ different to different people. ² Several years
                      taste

ago, scientists _____ different people with the same substance. ³To
               test

some it _____ bitter, while to others it _____ no taste at all.
        taste   have

⁴Another substance _____ sweet to some people but _____
                  taste   seem

bitter to others. ⁵These experiments _____ that there _____
                          show   be

four different taste classes among people. ⁶There _____ various
                                     be

"taste buds" located throughout the mouth. ⁷Taste _____ on these
                                   depend

taste buds—little bumps located on the tongue, cheeks, and throat. ⁸Those

on the tip of the tongue _____ sweetness. ⁹Those at the
                             designate

back _____ the bitter tastes. ¹⁰The cheeks _____ up sour
        catch   pick

tastes. ¹¹Flavor _____ also a very important factor of taste. ¹²Flavor
                be

_____ the eyes and nose in addition to the taste buds. ¹³In the
    use

past, I _____ no excuse for not eating something I _____.
        have   dislike

¹⁴Now, when I don't like something, I _____ it on my taste buds and
                                        blame

_____ to eat it.
    refuse

EXERCISE 4-C

Supply the correct present _or_ past _form of the verb or aux-word whose base form is beneath the blank._

TOOLS AND PROGRESS

¹One of the qualities that _____ men superior to the beasts
                          make

_____ their ability to make and use tools. ²Since early men's hands
    be

_____ not needed for moving around, they _____ them
    be   use

to carry and use tools. [3]The availability of their hands and their superior

intelligence _____ civilization and progress possible for men.
                make

[4]Men's first tools _____ primitive by today's standards. [5]A dead tree
                          be

branch _____ a tool for knocking fruit down from a tree. [6]Today, men
         become

_____ machines that _____ them up into the trees to pick
   have   lift

fruit easily and efficiently. [7]On some farms, machines _____ fruit and
                                                              harvest

vegetables all by themselves. [8]Men simply _____ these tools.
                                                   guide

[9]Primitive men also _____ their tools as weapons. [10]Many
                           use

centuries ago, men _____ heavy rocks to stout sticks and
                        attach

_____ clubs. [11]Attaching a sharpened rock to the end of a long, thin
   make

stick _____ in a spear. [12]Using these weapons _____ men to
         result   allow

kill strong animals and each other.

[13]Modern men _____ more sophisticated tools as weapons. [14]The
                     use

invention of gunpowder _____ a new era in weaponry. [15]Rifles
                             begin

and pistols _____ necessary tools for both soldiers and hunters.
                become

[16]Later men _____ more powerful explosives. [17]Today, men
                   develop

_____ the capacity to destroy themselves and the civilization that
   have

their hands and brains _____ centuries ago with the invention of
                             start

simple tools. [15]One only _____ that modern man's intelligence
                                hope

_____ greater than the destructive powers that he, with his tools,
   be

_____ .
   possess

5. The -ing Verb Form and Time

5.1   The timeless -ing verb form is used with the present tense aux-words *am, is,* and *are*
           to emphasize that an activity is **in progress** at the moment of speaking/writing.
           It may also indicate that the action is **repeated** many times.

> Mary is watching television.
> John is swimming in the pool.
> The movie is playing now.

5.2   The use of present tense aux-words with *-ing* verb forms may also indicate that an activity is considered **temporary** or **unusual**. In this case, they do not necessarily have to be taking place at the moment of speaking/writing, as long as they are **not customary**.

> I am having a lot of trouble this semester.
> The newspaper is presenting a series of John's articles.
> She is teaching a course in English at the college.
> The office is collecting funds for the Red Cross.

5.3   Future activities that are **planned** or **scheduled** may also be expressed by the use of the present tense aux-words *am, is,* and *are* plus the timeless *-ing* form of the verb when used with a **future time expression** such as *tomorrow, next year, this evening, tonight,* etc. (Compare with section 3.5 in this chapter.)

> We're going to Europe next summer.
> I'm having Bill and Mary over on Sunday.
> The boys on the team are giving a party this weekend.
> We're leaving on our vacation next week.
> I'm starting on a diet tomorrow.

5.4   The timeless *-ing* form of the verb is used with the past tense aux-words *was* and *were* to show:

1. activities **in progress at a specific time in the past**. Time expressions indicating a specific past time are generally used.

> It was raining last night.
> I was living in Syria at that time.
> They were having a lot of trouble last semester.

2. activities **in progress when another event occurs**. These in-progress activities usually serve as a background for another activity that is expressed in the simple past tense.

> I thought about her while I was walking home.
> The blowout occurred while we were passing another car.
> He was steering the boat when the wave turned it over.

5.5   In choosing the right tense/aspect, the most important consideration is what the speaker/writer is **thinking** or wants to **emphasize, not** the activity itself. For instance, aux + -*ing* can be used to emphasize that an activity is in progress, temporary, or unusual, even though the activity is normally considered habitual, customary, or a general truth.

The sun rises every day. (general truth, customary)
Look! The sun is rising. (right now, in progress, temporary)

The sun sets in the west. (general truth)
As the sun was slowly setting in the west, we finished the last chores of the day. (background)

Henry jogs every morning. (customary)
Henry isn't jogging today because he's sick. (unusual)

Note: The aux-word plus -*ing* verb form combinations are often called the present and past progressive tenses. Others call them the present and past continuous tenses.

EXERCISE 5-A

Supply the correct +s, no-s, past, base, or past/present aux (am, is, are, was, were) + -ing form of the verb or aux-word whose base form is shown beneath the blank.

RELAXING

¹Sometimes I just _____ to relax. ²I _____ my eyes
             like   close

and _____ my thoughts come and go. ³Sometimes someone
     let

_____ me and _____ me what I _____
  disturb   ask   do

or what I _____ of. ⁴Usually I _____ that I
        think   reply

_____ because that _____ much busier than
   meditate   sound

saying that I _____. ⁵Then people usually _____
        rest   leave

me alone although sometimes they _____ and _____.
           stop   talk

⁶Teachers and mothers simply do not _____. ⁷They
             understand

_____ all the time and _____ others need to
  work   think

_____ too. ⁸They _____ not very tolerant of laziness. ⁹Just last
  work   be

week, while I _____ on a chair, my mother quickly _____
     sit   find

a task to keep me busy because she _____ that I _____
        see   do

nothing. ¹⁰While I _____ I _____ that the next
     work   decide

time I _____ it would _____ somewhere
  rest   be

out of my mother's sight.

EXERCISE 5-B   *Supply the correct +s, no-s, past, base, or past/present aux (am, is, are, was, were) + -ing form of the verb or aux-word whose base form is shown beneath the blank.*

COSMIC COLLISIONS

¹You may _____ that the earth beneath your feet _____
think   be

stable, but in reality it _____ not. ²It _____ to be stationary,
be   seem

of course, but right now the earth _____ through space
move

at a tremendous speed, 66,600 miles per hour! ³It _____
revolve

on its axis also. ⁴Do you _____ that at this very moment you
realize

_____ around in circles at close to one thousand miles per
go

hour?

⁵Most people _____ no idea of the speed at which they
have

_____ through the universe. ⁶What they don't
travel

_____ doesn't _____ them. ⁷They _____
know   frighten   be

unaware that at the same time other objects, besides the planet earth,

_____ through space at fantastic speeds also. ⁸Nothing
hurtle

_____ these comets, meteors, planets, and stars from colliding with
prevent

each other. ⁹The only thing that _____ such collisions infrequent
make

_____ the immensity of space. ¹⁰The chances _____
be   be

small that one heavenly body will _____ into another one. ¹¹The
crash

results when they do, however, _____ disastrous. ¹²A meteorite once
be

_____ the earth in northern Arizona. ¹³It _____ a crater
hit   make

over 4,000 feet wide and nearly 600 feet deep. ¹⁴In 1908 a large meteorite

_____ into the earth in central Siberia. ¹⁵The resultant explosion
crash

_____ windows fifty miles away, _____ over eighty million
break   burn

trees, and _____ 1,500 reindeer.
kill

¹⁶People's ignorance of impending danger, although comforting, will not

_____ them from disaster. ¹⁷Knowing that a disaster
save

_____, however, _____ not much protection either.
approach   be

EXERCISE 5-C   *Supply the correct +s, no-s, past, base, or past/present aux (am, is, are, was, were)* + *-ing form of the verb or aux-word whose base form is shown beneath the blank.*

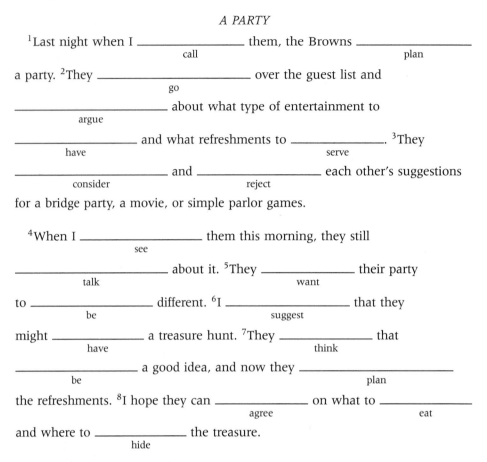

A PARTY

¹Last night when I _____ them, the Browns _____
                        call   plan

a party. ²They _____ over the guest list and
                        go

_____ about what type of entertainment to
      argue

_____ and what refreshments to _____. ³They
      have   serve

_____ and _____ each other's suggestions
      consider   reject

for a bridge party, a movie, or simple parlor games.

⁴When I _____ them this morning, they still
                see

_____ about it. ⁵They _____ their party
      talk   want

to _____ different. ⁶I _____ that they
      be   suggest

might _____ a treasure hunt. ⁷They _____ that
        have   think

_____ a good idea, and now they _____
      be   plan

the refreshments. ⁸I hope they can _____ on what to _____
                                          agree   eat

and where to _____ the treasure.
                  hide

6. The Earlier-Than-Established-Time Relationship

6.1   Once a present or past time has been established (by either a time expression or a verb form), related times—earlier and later aspects—are indicated by certain aux-word and timeless verb form combinations. The aux-words *have/has* are always followed by the timeless *d-t-n* form of a verb. This combination is used to show a time **earlier than the established present time**. The aux-word *had* followed by the *d-t-n* form is used to show a time earlier than the established past time.

6.2   This **earlier-than-the-present-time** aspect indicates...

1. that an activity existed or occurred "before now" at some (usually indefinite) time before the time of speaking/writing. The exact time is not always indicated, because it is not considered important. When this tense/aspect is used, it is usually difficult to answer the question "when?" with a specific time or date.

   Some common time expressions that indicate an action before the present time are *since, yet, already, ever,* and *for a long time.* Frequency words such as *several times, often, at last,* etc., may indicate one or more times.

> I have read that book several times.
> She has written three essays already.
> She has been at the university since last September.
> I have been here for too long.

The time expression *just* is often used to indicate or emphasize a very recent earlier time.

> We have just arrived.
> I have just returned from a trip to the Orient.

2. that an activity began in the past, has continued up to the present time, is still taking place, and will probably continue in the future.

> Today is October 27. Nancy got sick on October 13, and she is still sick. She has been sick for two weeks!
> I have listened to the choir broadcast for years.
> We have known those students for a long time.
> I have always liked that girl.
> Susan has been in Greece since she left here.

6.3   The **earlier-than-the-past-time** aspect indicates that an activity occurred or existed before another activity in the past.

> I had just finished my assignment when Bill arrived.
> I had already finished my homework when he invited me to go for a ride.
> I had never heard that story before I attended the lecture.
> I was irritable last Friday because I hadn't slept well the night before.

6.4   An earlier time reference may even become a new established time.

> Our plane left on July 12. We *had packed* our bags many days before. We didn't pack many things that we wanted to take because they didn't fit.

EXERCISE 6-A   *Supply the correct +s, no-*s, *past, base, be + ing, or* have/has *+ d-t-n form of the verb or aux-word whose base form is beneath the blank.*

MEXICAN EMPIRES—PART I

¹In the history of Mexico there _____ many empires. ²Most of
                                           be

these were Indian civilizations, which _____ and _____
                                                rise   fall

long before the arrival of the Spaniards. ³The last of these _____ the
                                                                be

Aztec empire, which Hernán Cortés _____ when he
                                          encounter

_____ the great central valley of Mexico in 1519.
      reach

⁴Before the Spanish arrived, the Aztecs _____ many
                                                 conquer

other Indian tribes. ⁵Building on the civilizations that _____
                                                            precede

them, they _____ their own empire. [6]Therefore, Aztec society
       create

_____ the achievements of other Indian societies that
   reflect

_____ before it—especially the Olmecs and the Mayas.
  go

  [7]The Olmec society _____ on the shores of the Gulf of Mexico
       arise

around 1200 B.C. [8]The Olmecs _____ large, raised,
     construct

rectangular courtyards. [9]They also _____ gigantic stone heads and
     carve

stone slabs decorated with figures of humans with jaguar faces. [10]The jaguar

_____ repeatedly in Olmec statuary and _____ in
  appear   *persist*

the religious art of other Indian societies for hundreds of years after the Olmecs

_____.
  vanish

  [11]The Mayas flourished in southeastern Mexico. [12]The origins of

their civilization _____ obscure. [13]Archeological discoveries
    be

_____, however, that by 300 A.D. the Mayas _____
  reveal   *begin*

constructing elaborate ceremonial centers. [14]Modern-day archaeologists

_____ evidence of the ceremonial nature of Mayan
    find

court life in tombs and buildings which they _____. [15]At
                               unearth

Bonampak, for example, visitors can _____ brilliantly executed
        see

murals which _____ the walls and ceilings of three rooms of a large
    cover

stone building. [16]One room _____ the preparations for a sacred
        show

ritual. [17]The second _____ a war party making a raid. [18]The third
     depict

_____ the execution and ritual sacrifice of the captives.
  illustrate

  [19]The Mayas also _____ various arts and sciences. [20]Mayan
       master

astronomers accurately _____ lunar phases, solar eclipses,
       calculate

and the orbits of other heavenly bodies. [21]The Mayas _____ a pictorial
        employ

writing system that _____ at least 800 different symbols. [22]They
    have

_____ them on paper made from tree bark and _____
  write   *carve*

them in stone. [23]In this way, they _____ an extensive record of their
                   leave

history.

EXERCISE 6-B   *Supply the correct +s, no-s, past, base, be + ing, or have/has + d-t-n form of the verb or aux-word whose base form is beneath the blank.*

MEXICAN EMPIRES—PART II

[1]While the Mayas _____ in southeastern Mexico, other Indian

live

civilizations _____ in the great Central Valley of Mexico. [2]Nomadic

rise

tribes occasionally _____ down from the highlands to the north and

sweep

_____ these civilizations.

conquer

[3]In the eleventh century, the Aztecs _____ this pattern.

follow

[4]They _____ from a mysterious land to the north which they

migrate

_____ Aztlán. [5]They _____ that they _____ a

call   believe   be

chosen people. [6]Before they left Aztlán, their god, Huitzilopochtli,

_____ to lead them to a place where they would find an eagle,

promise

perched on a cactus, with a snake in its beak. [7]In that place, the prophecies

_____, they would establish their new home.

foretell

[8]Around the year 1200, the Aztecs _____ in the Central Valley. [9]For

arrive

several generations they _____ the established Indian tribes. [10]Finally,

serve

in the year 1345, on an island in Lake Texcoco, they _____ their own

found

city and _____ it Tenochtitlán, "The Place of the Cactus."

call

[11]By 1428, the Aztecs _____ themselves as the dominant

establish

power in the region. [12]Not satisfied, they _____ on a vigorous policy

embark

of expansion. [13]By 1468, their empire _____ as far as Oaxaca and

expand

Veracruz. [14]In Tenochtitlán, the emperor Moctezuma I _____ architects

employ

to lay out streets and canals. [15]Stone buildings _____ adobe huts.

replace

[16]Gardens _____ everywhere. [17]An aqueduct _____ fresh

grow   bring

spring water into the city. [18]By the end of the fifteenth century, Tenochtitlán

_____ the richest and most beautiful city in Mexico, and perhaps in

become

the entire world.

[19]Moctezuma and his successors _____ in luxury. [20]However, in
live

the early sixteenth century a series of strange events _____ them
give

cause to worry. [21]One night a gigantic comet _____ in the sky. [22]One
appear

day, when there was no wind, an enormous wave _____ out of Lake
come

Texcoco and _____ many buildings along the shore. [23]Another
destroy

day, with no apparent cause, a temple _____ to the ground. [24]To the
burn

emperor's superstitious mind, these events _____ a great upheaval.
foretell

EXERCISE 6-C   *Supply the correct +s, no-s, past, base,* be + ing, *or* have/has + d-t-n *form of the verb or aux-word whose base form is beneath the blank.*

MEXICAN EMPIRES—PART III

[1]Early in 1519, a breathless messenger arrived in Tenochtitlán with the news

that strange tall ships _____ on the gulf coast. [2]The beings
arrive

on them _____ equally strange. [3]They _____
be   have

white skin and hairy faces. [4]They _____ suits of shining
wear

metal and _____ weapons that _____ fire and
use   spout

smoke. [5]Some of these weapons _____ so powerful they could
be

_____ a strong tree into splinters.
shatter

[6]To the Aztecs, these Europeans _____ more like gods
seem

than men. [7]Perhaps they _____ messengers preparing
be

the way for Quetzalcoatl, god of the morning star, who in ancient times

_____ to the East but who also _____ to
flee   promise

return.

[8]When Cortés and his men _____ in Tenochtitlán, on
arrive

November 8, 1519, Moctezuma _____ them a welcome
give

fit for gods. [9]A delegation of 4,000 nobles bearing garlands of flowers

_____ the Spaniards outside the city. [10]The emperor, under a
meet

canopy crafted of shining green feathers, pearls, and silver, _____
greet

them and _____ Cortés generous gifts of gold and silver.
offer

[11]The Spaniards _____ at the city. [12]It was far larger
$\quad$ marvel

than Seville, one of the great cities of Europe, which Cortés and his men

_____ a few months before. [13]Tenochtitlán _____
$\quad$ leave $\qquad$ have

clean streets, lovely gardens, a zoo with a variety of exotic animals, many

palaces, and a grand temple.

[14]The Aztecs, however, soon _____ suspicious about the true
$\qquad$ become

motives of the Spanish. [15]Feeling threatened, the Spanish _____
$\qquad$ take

Moctezuma hostage. [16]Cortés and his men _____ themselves
$\qquad$ find

surrounded by hostile Aztec warriors. [17]When Moctezuma _____,
$\qquad$ die

the Spanish situation _____ hopeless, but on July 1, 1520,
$\qquad$ seem

Cortés and about half of his men _____ to escape from
$\qquad$ manage

Tenochtitlán. [18]They later _____ with reinforcements and full-
$\qquad$ return

scale war _____ out between the Spanish and the Aztecs. [19]By
$\qquad$ break

the end of the war, thousands of Spanish and Indians _____
$\qquad$ die

in battles and from disease and starvation. [20]By the time it _____
$\qquad$ be

over, the Spanish cannons _____ the great city of
$\qquad$ reduce

Tenochtitlán to rubble. [21]To give themselves room to maneuver, the invaders

_____ the city. [22]They _____ the buildings, the
$\quad$ level $\qquad$ destroy

gardens, and the zoo, and they _____ the temple. [23]By the
$\qquad$ burn

year 1521, the Aztec empire, the last of the great Mexican Indian civilizations,

_____ and Mexico _____ a vassal to Spain.
$\quad$ fall $\qquad$ become

EXERCISE 6.1-A   *Supply the correct +s, no-s, past, base, or* have/has *or* had + d-t-n *form of the verb*
or aux-word whose base form is beneath the blank.

NOAH'S ARK? PART I*

[1]Most people in the world today _____ the story of
$\qquad$ hear

Noah's Ark. [2]Relatively few of them _____, however, that
$\qquad$ know

for many years there _____ reports that a large structure that
$\qquad$ be

*(Information for these three passages has been taken from *In Search of Noah's Ark* by Dave Balsiger
and Charles E. Sellier, Jr.)

_____ like a boat _____ buried beneath ice
   look   lie

and snow at the 14,000-foot level on Mount Ararat in Eastern Turkey.

[3]The structure _____ as large as modern battleships, but it
               be

_____ made of wood. [4]Whenever they _____
  be   hear

these reports, many people _____ that Noah's Ark
                      believe

_____ found.
  be

[5]Since 700 B.C., historians and explorers _____ such a
                             mention

structure on Mt. Ararat. [6]In 1840, a Turkish expedition which

_____ checking for damage caused by an earthquake that
  be

_____ earlier that year _____ a gigantic
  occur   discover

wooden ship on Mt. Ararat. [7]Some men even _____ plans to
                          make

_____ the structure and _____ it at the 1893
  excavate   exhibit

World's Fair in Chicago.

[8]In 1970, an old man named George Hagopian _____ that 68
                               claim

years earlier he _____ the Ark. [9]He _____ that
          visit   report

his uncle _____ him up and he _____ on the
      lift   walk

roof of the Ark.

EXERCISE 6.1-B   *Supply the correct +s, no-s, past, base, or have/has or had + d-t-n form of the verb or aux-word whose base form is beneath the blank.*

NOAH'S ARK? PART II

[1]Since the turn of the century other expeditions _____ the
                            make

difficult journey up Mt. Ararat also. [2]They _____ Mt. Ararat
                      find

to _____ treacherous. [3]Nearly every day, storms and blizzards
  be

_____ on the mountain. [4]Avalanches _____
  occur   kill

many climbers.

[5]In the past few decades, several earthquakes _____ in
                      occur

Eastern Turkey. [6]Some Ark experts _____ that these earthquakes
                   report

_____ the wooden structure into several pieces. [7]Some of these
  break

pieces _____ from their original position to other locations
      slip

farther down the mountain where they _____ more accessible.

become

[8]By late 1955, a French explorer named Fernand Navarra _____

recover

wood from the structure. [9]Modern dating tests conducted since then

_____ that the wood _____ thousands of years old.

reveal   be

[10]In recent years some critics _____ fault with the reports of

find

people who _____ the site where the structure _____

visit   be

located. [11]However, they cannot _____ that since 1856 over two

deny

hundred people on twenty-three different occasions _____ seeing

report

the structure on Mt. Ararat.

EXERCISE 6.1-C *Supply the correct +s, no-s, past, base, or* have/has *or* had + d-t-n *form of the verb or aux-word whose base form is beneath the blank.*

NOAH'S ARK? PART III

[1]Today, exploration of Mount Ararat _____ not allowed. [2]In

be

1974, Turkish government officials _____ regulations prohibiting

announce

foreigners from traveling to Mt. Ararat. [3]Since then, they _____

give

a number of reasons for these regulations.

[4]On several occasions they _____ that the Russians

explain

_____ a military missile facility only forty miles from

build

the mountain across the Turkish-Soviet border. [5]This development

_____ Mt. Ararat to be classified as a restricted military zone.

cause

[6]Although travel to Mt. Ararat _____ prohibited, for the past few

be

years many adventurers _____ to _____

continue   make

plans to _____ the mountain when the ban is lifted. [7]One

visit

explorer named McCollum _____ his plan to use a large

announce

helicopter to _____ supplies and equipment to the site. [8]He

airlift

_____ to _____ the helicopter to the Turkish

promise   donate

government once the expedition _____ its purpose, but

accomplish

his plan _____ to receive Turkish approval. [9]Since he originally

fail

_____ the expedition in 1970, McCollum _____

plan   sell

his large helicopter, but he _____ still ready, for he
be

_____ it with another helicopter which _____
replace   have

even more horsepower. [10]He still _____ to prove beyond doubt
hope

that the structure on Mt. Ararat _____ really Noah's Ark.
be

7. The Later-Than-Established-Time Relationship

7.1 The **later-than-the-present-established-time** relationship is expressed by using the aux-word *will* (or *shall*) or the phrase *am/is/are going to* plus the base form of the verb. This tense/aspect indicates that an activity is expected to happen **after** the established present time.

We *hope* they *will leave* soon.
(established   (later time)
present)

I *can't do* it now, but I *will do* it later.
(established   (later time)
present)

He *will fail* if he *doesn't study*.
(later time)   (present time)

He *is going to leave* tomorrow.
(later time)

I *am going to do* my homework in a few minutes.
(later time)

- To make a **prediction**, either *will* or *be + going to* can be used.
- To describe **planned activities**, only *be + going to* should be used.
- To show **willingness** to do something, make **promises**, extend **invitations**, and express **desires**, only *will* should be used.

7.2 The **later-than-the-past-established-time** relationship is shown by using the aux-word *would* or the phrase *was/were going to* plus the base form of the verb.

Last night he *promised* he *would help* us tomorrow.
(established past)   (later time)   (later time)

Yesterday, he *said* he *was going to do* it.
(established past)   (later time)

This morning they *told* us they *were going to visit* Hawaii next summer.
(established past)   (later time)   (later time)

The later time in the past can extend **beyond the present** into the future.

Five years ago he *predicted* that the world *would end* in 1999.
(established past)   (later time)

Note: The modal *would* is also frequently used to show unreal conditions (section 11) and customary activity in the past (section 4.2) (see also Chapter 4, section 8.2).

7.3   A later time reference may become a new established time.

> Joe *said* he *would call* me after the game, and he *didn't forget*.
> (est. past)   (later time)   (new established time)

EXERCISE 7-A   *Supply the correct +s, no-s, past, base, have/has or had + d-t-n form, will, would + base form, or is/am/are, was/were going to + base form of the verb or aux-word whose base form is beneath the blank.*

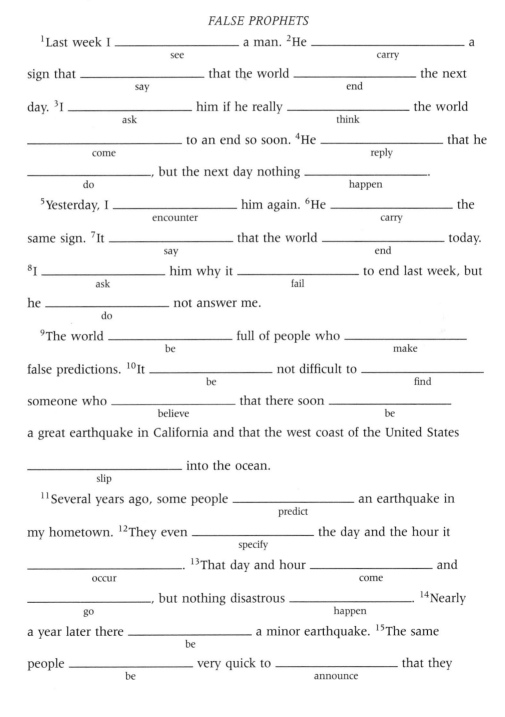

FALSE PROPHETS

[1]Last week I _____ a man. [2]He _____ a
                          see   carry
sign that _____ that the world _____ the next
              say   end
day. [3]I _____ him if he really _____ the world
              ask   think
_____ to an end so soon. [4]He _____ that he
      come   reply
_____, but the next day nothing _____.
      do   happen

[5]Yesterday, I _____ him again. [6]He _____ the
                    encounter   carry
same sign. [7]It _____ that the world _____ today.
                        say   end
[8]I _____ him why it _____ to end last week, but
        ask   fail
he _____ not answer me.
      do

[9]The world _____ full of people who _____
                    be   make
false predictions. [10]It _____ not difficult to _____
                                be   find
someone who _____ that there soon _____
                      believe   be
a great earthquake in California and that the west coast of the United States

_____ into the ocean.
      slip

[11]Several years ago, some people _____ an earthquake in
                                              predict
my hometown. [12]They even _____ the day and the hour it
                                        specify
_____. [13]That day and hour _____ and
      occur   come
_____, but nothing disastrous _____. [14]Nearly
      go   happen
a year later there _____ a minor earthquake. [15]The same
                              be
people _____ very quick to _____ that they
              be   announce

_____ it _____, but everybody just
   predict   happen

laughed. [16]It _____ no special talent to _____ an
              take   predict

event after it _____.
              happen

EXERCISE 7-B   *Supply the correct +s, no-s, past, base,* have/has *or* had + d-t-n *form,* will, would + *base form, or* is/am/are, was/were going to + *base form of the verb or aux-word whose base form is beneath the blank.*

AN ASTRONAUT

[1]The first time I _____ an astronaut on television, I _____
                    see   hope

that someday I _____ one. [2]When I _____ news
              become   watch

broadcasts about space flights, I _____ that NASA _____
                       dream   invite

me to _____ along on the next space voyage. [3]I _____
   go   imagine

how great it _____ to _____ weightlessly through
          be   soar

space. [4]I _____ there _____ nothing to _____
         think   be   do

but relax and enjoy myself. [5]However, when I _____ a space
                                see

capsule for the first time, I _____ my mind. [6]Now I no longer
                   change

_____ to _____ an astronaut, as astronauts _____
 want   become   have

more to _____ than I _____. [7]When an astronaut
        do   have

_____ into orbit, I _____ he _____ less sleep
  go   know   get

than I _____ now. [8]He _____ to _____
      do   have   be

alert. [9]Quarters _____ crowded. [10]It _____ more
           be   take

effort to _____ things in the capsule. [11]Without gravity, nothing
     do

_____ put. [12]He _____ to _____ on or
 stay   have   hang

_____ strapped down to _____ in one place. [13]Although
 be   stay

previously I _____ I _____ my troubles by leaving the earth,
         think   escape

now I _____ I _____ to _____ of some new way
     know   have   think

to _____ away from it all.
  get

EXERCISE 7-C *Supply the correct +s, no-s, past, base,* have/has *or* had + d-t-n *form,* will, would + *base form, or* is/am/are, was/were going to + *base form of the verb or aux-word whose base form is beneath the blank.*

DOOMSDAY!

¹Many people _____ that men _____
　　　　　　　　　　　think　　　　　　　　　　　　　　destroy
themselves eventually. ²Some _____ atomic wars whichnl
　　　　　　　　　　　　　　　forecast
_____ this planet. ³Others _____ that
　　　　devastate　　　　　　　　　　　　　　　predict
society's pollution _____ modern civilization. ⁴According
　　　　　　　　　　　　destroy
to these people, smog, oil spills, the leakage of stored chemicals, and the like

_____ man's doom. ⁵Some _____ that the
　　　be　　　　　　　　　　　　　　　　feel
moral breakdown of society _____ man to an animal state.
　　　　　　　　　　　　　　　reduce
⁶Others _____ to the increasing frequency and severity of
　　　　　　　point
natural disasters—earthquakes, hurricanes, winter storms, tidal waves, etc.—

and _____ that nature _____ man's fragile
　　　　say　　　　　　　　　　　　overthrow
civilization.

　　⁷Predictors of destruction _____ not new, of course. ⁸Almost
　　　　　　　　　　　　　　　be
as soon as civilization _____ people _____ to
　　　　　　　　　　start　　　　　　　　　begin
_____ that it _____.
　　predict　　　　　　　　end
⁹No one really _____ how or when the world
　　　　　　　　　know
_____. ¹⁰When we _____ out, it
　　end　　　　　　　　　　find
_____ too late.
　be

8. Summary of Time and Tense Relationships

The following diagrams illustrate the different time relationships with their corresponding verb forms that have been discussed in the last two sections (6 and 7).

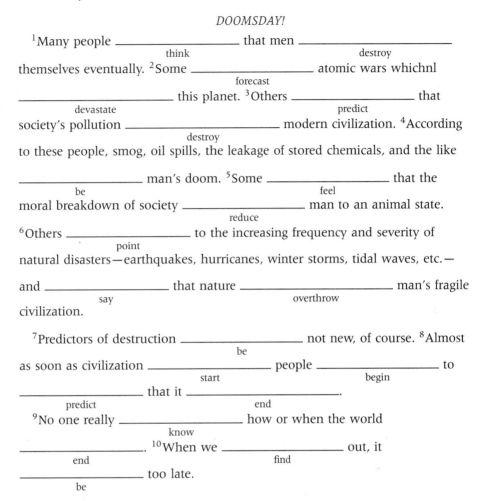

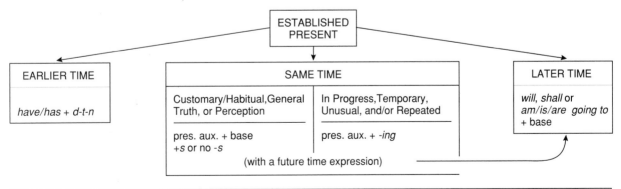

I am lost in the desert. I am crawling across the sand. I see mirages everywhere. I have not had a drink of water for two days. I think I am going to die. I hope someone will rescue me.

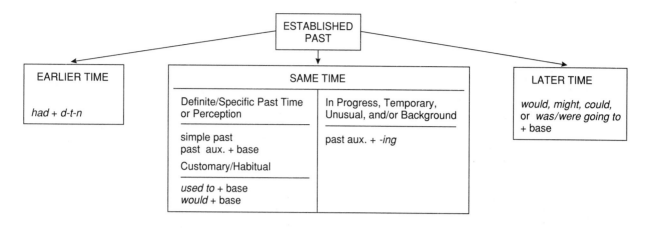

Last month, I was lost in the desert. I was crawling across the sand. I saw mirages everywhere. I had not had a drink of water for two days. I thought I was going to die. I hoped someone would rescue me, and somebody did.

Now, referring to the previous diagrams, study the following examples:

John Jones *works* for an international corporation.	PRESENT TIME established by *works*
He *has recently* returned from a business trip to Japan.	*has* and *recently* show earlier-than-established-time
He *is going* to report to the corporation's board of directors	*is going to* shows later-than-established-time
at their *next* meeting, which *will* be held *next* Thursday.	*next*, *next Thursday*, and *will* show later-than-established-time
Before he *was* hired for this assignment, he *had* traveled widely in the Middle East.	PAST TIME established by *was*; *had* shows earlier-than-established-time;
Recommendations from his previous employer *state*,	PRESENT TIME established by *state*, which indicates a statement of fact
"Mr. Jones *has served* the firm faithfully and diligently during the *past two years*."	*has* shows earlier-than-established-time; *past two years* shows earlier-than-established-time
Last week, when I *talked* to Mr. Jones about speaking to our business students,	PAST TIME established by *Last week*; *talked* shows same established time
he *said*	*said* shows same as established time
he *would* be happy to explain the challenges of intercultural business to us.	*would* shows later-than-established-time

9. Later or Earlier Time with *-ing* Forms

Later and earlier relationships of activities in progress can be shown by a **combination** of the normal earlier (*has/have; had*) or later (*will, would; am/is/are going to, was/were going to*) aux-words plus *been* or *be* followed by an *-ing* verb form.

> I *have been reading* this book for hours.
> (earlier-than-present time,
>   in progress)
>
> I *will be going* home soon.
> (later-than-present time,
>   in progress)
>
> Before I helped him yesterday, John *had been trying* to fix the car for hours.
> (earlier-than-past time,
>   in progress)
>
> He said he *would have been working* on it forever if someone hadn't helped him.
> (later-than-past time,
>   in progress)

EXAMPLE PARAGRAPH:

I saw Jennifer at the corner yesterday. She was waiting for Mike. She *had been waiting* for nearly an hour. She said she *was going to wait* another five minutes. Then she *would be leaving*.

Here is a longer example from American literature that illustrates time relationships (same, earlier, and later; simple and in-progress) well.

THE PEARL*

In the town they *tell* the story of the great pearl....	*tell* establishes present time
They *tell* of Kino the fisherman, and his wife, Juana, and of the baby Coyotito.	*tell* shows same time in present
And because the story *has been told* so often, it *has taken* root in every man's mind....	*has been told* and *has taken root* show time earlier than the time of telling (established present)
Kino *awakened* in the near dark.	*awakened* establishes a new, past time
The stars still *shone* and the day *had drawn* only a pale wash of light in the lower sky to the east.	*shone* = same time as *awakened* *had drawn* = earlier than *awakened*
The Roosters *had been crowing* for some time, and the early pigs *were* already *beginning* their ceaseless turning of twigs and bits of wood to see whether anything to eat *had been overlooked*.	*had been crowing* = earlier than *awakened*, in progress *were beginning* = same time as *awakened*, in progress *had been overlooked* = earlier time than *awakened*
Outside the brush house in the tuna clump, a covey of little birds *chittered* and *flurried* with their wings.	*chittered* and *flurried* = same time as *awakened*
Kino *heard* the little splash of morning waves on the beach.	*heard* = same time as *awakened* (or new established time, slightly later)
It *was* very good. Kino *closed* his eyes again to listen to his music. Perhaps he alone *did* this and perhaps all of his people *did* it.	*was, closed,* and *did* = same time as *heard*
His people *had* once *been* great makers of songs so that everything they *saw* or *thought* or *did* or *heard* *became* a song.	*had once been* = earlier time (indefinite past) *saw, thought, did, heard, became* = same time as *heard* (customary/habitual) or *thought*

*John Steinbeck, *The Pearl* (New York: Viking, 1947). Used by permission.

10. Modal + *have* Combinations

Sometimes the timeless aux-word *have* (followed by the *d-t-n* form of a verb) comes after a modal. This combination **cannot** be used for all meanings of the modals (see Chapter 4, section 8). For example, the modal *must* has two meanings:

> **necessity**   You must do your homework.   (It is a requirement.)
> **probability**   You must be smart.   (You are learning very quickly.)

When *must* is used to show necessity, it **cannot** be followed by *have* + *d-t-n*. Adding *have* changes the meaning of necessity to probability (based on a logical conclusion).

> **probability**   You must have done your homework.
> (You got a good grade.)

The listing below shows which modals can be followed by *have* + *d-t-n* and which meanings are changed. An asterisk (*) indicates that adding *have* changes the meaning. A double asterisk (**) indicates that *have* cannot be added because the resulting combination is not semantically appropriate.

Modal and Meaning	Without *have*	With *have*
can ability inability possibility request	Bill can swim. John can't do it. It can get cold here at times. Can you help me?	** John can't have done it. ** **
could ability possibility/probability request	Joan could write well. We could eat at a restaurant. He asked me if I could go with him.	*(to possibility/probability) We could have eaten at a restaurant. *(to possibility/probability)
may possibility permission	He may be the man you're after. May I go now?	He may have been the man you're after. **
might possibility	John might get the job.	John might have gotten the job.
must necessity probability	You must work hard to get ahead. She must be your girlfriend.	*(to probability) She must have been your girlfriend.
should advisability probability	He should pay his taxes. The oranges should be ripe by now.	He should have paid his taxes. The oranges should have been ripe by now.
will request later time	Will you do it? He will finish by tomorrow.	** He will have finished by tomorrow.
would request habitual past possibility/probability	Would you come with me? When we were young we would often miss school. If I had their address, I would write them a letter.	*(to possibility) *(to possibility) If I had had their address, I would have written them a letter.

EXERCISE 10-A   *In the blanks in the passage below, supply appropriate aux-word and verb form combinations. Use the modal +* have *+ d-t-n combination when it is called for.*

A STRANGE SIGHT

[1]When I saw Mr. Finstrom the other day, he was in a funny position. [2]His head and shoulders were inside his house, but his feet were sticking out the window.

[3]I didn't know what _____, but I used my imagination

happen

and came up with several possibilities. [4]He _____

sneak

out of the house and avoiding the front door. [5]On the other hand, he

_____ the house through the window because

enter

he _____ or lost his house key. [6]There were

forgotten

some other, more imaginative possibilities as well. [7]Perhaps some

gangsters _____ his family hostage and they

take

_____ them in the living room. [8]In that case, Mr.

hold

Finstrom _____ through the window on his way to get

escape

help. [9]He and his wife _____ an argument. [10]If so, she

have

_____ the door shut to keep him out.

nail

[11]As it turned out, the answer was not nearly that unusual. [12]Mr. Finstrom

_____ some people to paint the inside of his house.

hire

[13]As professional painters, they _____ better, but

know

they _____ when they painted the inside of the door

not think

frames. [14]They _____ and _____

finish   _leave_

the house earlier in the day. [15]By the time Mr. Finstrom got home, the

paint _____ and the doors were stuck. [16]The doors

dry

_____ because of the glue-like paint. [17]Crawling through

not open

the window was the only way he _____ into the

get

house.

EXERCISE 10-B   *In the blanks in the passage below, supply appropriate aux-word and verb form combinations. Use the modal +* have + *d-t-n combination when it is called for.*

A TRAFFIC ACCIDENT

[1]There was an automobile accident near school early this morning. [2]Like all accidents, it _____ , but it did. [3]The driver of one car
_{not happen}

had a hard time believing that the accident _____ at
_{happen}

all. [4]He kept walking around with his hands on his head, repeating, "This

_____ to me. [5]Things like this happen to other people,
_{not happen}

but *not* to me." [6]The driver of the other car assured him that, without a doubt,

it really _____ . [7]The investigating policeman kept asking
_{happen}

what _____ , but he couldn't get a straight story.
_{happen}

[8]The first driver admitted that he _____ more attention
_{pay}

to driving but that he _____ of something else. [9]He
_{think}

couldn't remember what it was that he _____ about.
_{think}

[10]My first impression was that the second driver _____
_{be}

drunk. [11]He shouted and got red as if he _____ , but later I
_{drink}

decided that he _____ upset and not drunk. [12]He insisted
_{be}

that the accident was not his fault, but the policeman seemed to think that

he _____ the other car if he _____
_{avoid}   _{drive}

defensively. [13]Obviously, he _____ for the other guy
_{not look out}

like he _____ , but I couldn't see how the accident
_{be}

_____ his fault. [14]At any rate, I'm not the judge.
_{be}

[15]Perhaps by now, the policeman _____ exactly
_{figure out}

what happened and who was at fault. [16]By tomorrow, the accident

_____ just one more traffic statistic.
_{become}

EXERCISE 10-C   *In the blanks in the passage below, supply appropriate aux-word and verb form combinations. Use the modal + have + d-t-n combination when it is called for.*

A MURDER MYSTERY

[1]The murder was a terrible thing, but it seemed even worse because no one

had any idea who _____ it. [2]It _____

commit   be

the butler. [3]Butlers are always prime suspects, but he had a good alibi. [4]Some

people _____ the victim's wife, but there were witnesses

accuse

who _____ with her at the time of the crime. [5]Therefore,

be

it was concluded that she _____ guilty. [6]The detectives

not be

thought that a suspicious neighbor _____ the murder, but

commit

they had no proof.

[7]The cause of death was even more elusive. [8]There was no doubt

that the victim was dead, but there were no indications of what

_____ him to die. [9]There were no marks on the body,

cause

but the murderer _____ poison. [10]That possibility could not

use

be ruled out until after the coroner _____ an autopsy. [11]By

perform

then, however, the guilty party _____.

escape

[12]The detectives couldn't wait that long. [13]They investigated further and found

a clue they _____ before. [14]It was good they didn't give up.

overlook

[15]Otherwise, they never _____ it. [16]This clue led to others

find

until the persistent detectives _____ the mystery.

solve

11. Real and Unreal Conditions

11.1   Some sentences consist of two parts or clauses: one which shows a condition and another which shows a result. (Sometimes there is more than one result clause.) The condition clause does not always come first in the sentence, but you can recognize it because it starts with a word or phrase like *if* or *unless*.

11.2 The condition clause may express an idea which is **real, possible, factual,** or **true**. Normal **present tense verb forms** (with earlier or later time as appropriate) are used in this case.

Condition Clause (Real)	Result Clause
Unless you study,	you will fail this class.
In the event that she needs money,	give her this twenty-dollar bill.
If you help me now,	I will help you later.
If you eat too much,	you will gain weight.

11.3 The condition clause may also express an idea which is **unreal, contrary to fact, imaginary,** or **hypothetical**. To show this unreal condition, **past-tense verb forms** are used in the condition clause, and the aux-word *would*, followed by the base form of the verb, is used in the result clause, even though the time is present.

Condition Clause (Unreal)	Result Clause
If you studied more,	you would do better
(Reality: You don't study enough. You are doing poorly.)	
If she needed money,	I would give her this twenty-dollar bill.
(Reality: She doesn't need money. I will keep this twenty-dollar bill.)	
If you helped me,	I would help you.
(Reality: You are not helping me. I will not help you.)	
If you ate less,	you would not be overweight.
(Reality: You eat too much. You are overweight.)	

The following two example sentences illustrate the difference between real and unreal conditions. In which case should you expect to receive any money?

> 1. If I have the money, I will give it to you.
> 2. If I had the money, I would give it to you.

You can expect to receive money only in the first case. (Of course, it is still only a possibility, depending on the condition that the money is available.) In the second case, the message is "I don't have the money." (So don't expect me to give it to you.) *If I had the money* is a contrary-to-fact, hypothetical condition. It may look like past tense, but it is really *present-unreal*.

11.4 When the unreal condition clause uses a form of *be* (*was* or *were*), it is proper to use *were* even though the subject is singular, *you*, or *I*. (Normally, these subjects would take the aux-word *was*.)

If I *were* you,	I would get out of here.
If Mr. Jones *were* wise,	he would invest his money with me.

11.5   To show **unreal conditions in the past**, use the aux-word *had* (followed by the *d-t-n* form of the verb) in the condition clause and the aux-words *would have* followed by the *d-t-n* form of the verb) in the result clause.

> If Sam had gone to the doctor earlier,   he would have suffered less.
>   (Reality: Sam did not go to the doctor earlier, and he suffered.)
> If I had known he was listening,   I would not have said anything.
>   (Reality: I did not know he was listening, and I said something.)
> If he had invested his money with me,   he would have been rich.
>   (Reality: He did not invest his money with me, and he isn't rich.)

Sentences like these use verb forms which may look like earlier past time, but the meaning is **past-unreal**.

11.6   The following chart summarizes the preceding discussion. You may want to refer to it as you do the exercises for this section.

| TIME | REAL | | UNREAL | |
	Condition	Result	Condition	Result
Present	If I study more, (simple present tense and present/future time)	I will receive higher grades. (*will* + base form)	If I studied more, (past tense form but present time)	I would receive higher grades. (*would* + base form) (Reality: I don't, so I won't.)
Past	(My teacher said that . . .) if I studied more, (simple past tense and past time)	I would receive higher grades. (*would* + base form)	If I had studied more, (*had* + *d-t-n* form, but simple past time)	I would have received higher grades. (*would* + *have* + *d-t-n* form) (Reality: I didn't.)

EXERCISE 11-A   *Read each sentence below and determine whether the conditions expressed are real or unreal. If they are real, write* R *by the number. If they are unreal, write* U *and then rewrite the sentence to express the reality.*

MY DAY

1. If I wake up on time, I will not get behind schedule today.

2. If I eat a good breakfast, I will have more energy throughout the morning.

3. If I take too long to eat, however, I will be late to work.

4. If I had time, I would take the scenic route to work.

5. If I get to work late, the boss will be angry.

6. If the boss gets angry with me one more time, I might get fired.

7. If I get to work on time and work hard, I will finish early, the boss will be happy, and I will have more time for lunch.

8. If I have time, I will find a quiet spot, put my feet up, and relax.

9. If I fall asleep, I may not wake up in time to get back to work.

10. If the weather were good, I could take a leisurely stroll in the park.

11. If it were summer, there might be flowers to see and smell.

12. If I took too long in the park and got back late, however, I would probably lose my job.

13. If my boss weren't so concerned about punctuality, my life would be more pleasant.

EXERCISE 11-B   *Read each sentence below and determine whether the conditions expressed are real or unreal. If they are real, write* R *by the number. If they are unreal, write* U *and then rewrite the sentence to express the reality.*

A SCHOLAR'S LAMENT

1. If I had taken more difficult classes in high school, I would have been better prepared for university courses.

2. If I had studied more for my last history test, I wouldn't have failed it.

3. If my mind had been rested, I might have been able to answer more questions correctly.

4. If I do better on the next test, I can still get a decent grade in history.

5. If I stay up late, I will be able to review for the test.

6. If I don't get enough sleep, however, I may fall asleep during the test.

7. If I prepare well for one class, I neglect the others.

8. If I hadn't signed up for so many courses, I could focus my attention better.

9. If my teachers didn't assign so much homework, I would have time to think about what I am learning.

10. If I had signed up for some easier classes, I wouldn't have so many research papers to write.

11. If the books I need aren't in the library, I won't be able to write my papers.

12. Even if I do find the books, I will have to spend many hours reading them and writing my papers.

13. If only I had more time, I could do everything I need to do.

EXERCISE 11-C *Read each sentence below and determine whether the conditions expressed are real or unreal. If they are real, write* R *by the number. If they are unreal, write* U *and then rewrite the sentence to express the reality.*

AN UPSETTING EXPERIENCE

1. If you think I look upset, I will tell you why.

2. If I hadn't gone to the baseball game with my neighbor George last night, I would have been in a better mood this morning.

3. If the home team had played better, they would have won.

4. If our outfielders had not dropped so many fly balls, the visiting team would not have scored so many points.

5. If our pitcher had a stronger arm, the visitors would not have hit so many home runs.

6. If our star player had controlled his temper, he wouldn't have been thrown out of the game.

7. If the umpire hadn't been blind, he wouldn't have made so many bad calls.

8. If I hadn't bet so much money on the home team, I would not have lost so much.

9. If George asks me to go to next week's game, I will tell him I'm busy.

10. If he wants to bet on the outcome, I will tell him, "Forget it."

EXERCISE 11.1-A   *In the blanks in the passage below, supply appropriate aux-words and aux-word +*
verb combinations to show real and unreal conditions as appropriate.

THE END OF THE WORLD

^{1}Every morning I turn on the radio and listen to the news. ^{2}It _____
help

me plan my day ^{3}If the traffic _____ bad on the highway I normally
be

_____, I _____ an alternate route to the office. ^{4}If the
use   take

weather forecast _____ for rain, I _____ an umbrella along.
be   take

^{5}If the news broadcast _____ me that the earth was going to collide
tell

with a giant asteroid in twenty-four hours, I _____ shocked. ^{6}At
be

first, I _____ it. ^{7}If I _____ something like that
not believe   hear

I _____ that it was some sick person's idea of a joke.
suspect

^{8}If the report _____ true, however, I _____
be   not do

the things I do on a normal day. ^{9}I _____ my last twenty-
live

four hours differently. ^{10}I _____ to the office. ^{11}No, if today
not go

_____ my last day on earth, I _____ it with the
be   spend

ones I love the most. ^{12}I _____ my family together.
gather

^{13}If the world _____ going to be destroyed tomorrow, we
be

_____ far from the city. ^{14}We _____ some quiet
go   find

spot with beautiful flowers and shade trees. ^{15}We _____
listen

to the birds sing and _____ the warmth of the sunshine.
enjoy

^{16}We _____ our feelings for each other and our
express

gratitude for the good life we _____ together. ^{17}We
enjoy

_____ to leave this world with happy memories, if it
want

_____ going to end tomorrow.
be

EXERCISE 11.1-B   *In the blanks in the passage below, supply appropriate aux-words and aux-word +*
verb combinations to show real and unreal conditions as appropriate.

PAY DAY DREAMING

¹Last week I got my first paycheck. ²I said to myself: "If I _____
                                                                         spend

this money wisely, I _____ some left over. ³If I
                              have

_____ it wisely, it _____—slowly but surely. ⁴On
       invest   grow

the other hand, if I _____ a lottery ticket, I _____ big right
                           buy   win

away. ⁵If I _____ the lottery, I _____
                   win   retire

early and see the world."

⁶I decided to buy the ticket. ⁷Unfortunately, I did not win. ⁸If I

_____ the million-dollar prize, I _____
           win   buy

a yacht. ⁹In my yacht I _____ around the world. ¹⁰I
                                  sail

_____ Tahiti, Australia, Japan, and Alaska one year. ¹¹Then
         visit

I _____ south and _____ the coast of
         turn   tour

Latin America. ¹²The following year I _____ the Atlantic
                                                 sail

Ocean and the Mediterranean. ¹³I _____ the Indian Ocean
                                          save

for last. ¹⁴When I was finished sailing, I _____ the yacht
                                                    sell

and _____ a house in the mountains.
         buy

¹⁵But, of course, all that was a dream. ¹⁶I didn't win. ¹⁷Now if I

_____ dreaming, I _____ my work.
      not stop   never finish

¹⁸If I _____ on time, I _____ my job.
             not finish   lose

¹⁹Then I _____ any more paychecks.
              not receive

EXERCISE 11.1-C   *In the blanks in the passage below, supply appropriate aux-words and aux-word +*
verb combinations to show real and unreal conditions as appropriate.

A MENTAL GAME

¹I seem to be accident prone. ²I don't know why I have more accidents than

other people do. ³That's just the way I am.

⁴My mother used to tell me, "You're not careful enough. ⁵If you

_____ more careful, you _____ so
         be   not have

many accidents." ⁶My father would say, "You run too fast. ⁷If you

_____ so fast you _____ into so many
             not run   not bump

things."

    ⁸I haven't learned to avoid accidents, but I have learned to play the "if

only" game in my mind. ⁹For example, last Tuesday, after I broke my nose

on a door, I said to myself, "If only I _____ where I was
                                                look

going, I _____ that the door was closed." ¹⁰Yesterday,
                 notice

after I wrecked my car, I thought, "I _____ that wrong
                                     not make

turn if only I _____ the street sign that said 'One Way.' "
                   notice

    ¹¹This morning I threw away the report I had worked on all night long

and handed in the newspaper. ¹²How embarrassing! ¹³I thought, "If only I

_____ more attention to what I was doing when I walked past
         pay

the trash can, I _____ away the wrong paper."
                    not throw

    ¹⁴Of course, mental torture like this does not change the past. ¹⁵My

car is still wrecked, my nose still hurts, and I have to rewrite my report.

    ¹⁶Nevertheless, I hope that if I _____ the "if only" game enough I
                                  play

_____ to be careful and avoid at least some accidents. ¹⁷If I
             learn

_____ able to do that, my life _____ much
       be   be

more pleasant.

12. Proofreading

As explained previously, an important part of the process of writing is proofreading. Although you now have a better understanding of how English aux-words and verbs are used to show different times and time relationships, you may still make occasional mistakes with them.

    The following exercises will give you practice in focused proofreading. The passages contain numerous mistakes with aux-words and verbs and the times they indicate, but that is the only type of error they contain. Using what you have learned in this chapter, focus on finding and fixing the incorrect aux-words and verbs.

EXERCISE 12-A

In the paragraphs below, there are a number of errors involving verb forms and the times they indicate (inappropriate switching between past and present, disagreement with the time signal, wrong tense for the time implied, etc.). Find the errors, correct them, and then rewrite the passage. Do not add, remove, or change any words except aux-words and verb forms.

A DISASTROUS GAME—PART I

[1]State University has a good football team this year and hoped to win the conference championship. [2]Most of the players have had great natural talent, and in high school several of them were star athletes. [3]Nevertheless, they hadn't rested on their laurels. [4]Since the pre-season practices, they worked hard to increase their strength and improve their skills.

[5]It is not surprising, then, that the SU team won most of its games this season. [6]The few games it lost have been with top teams, and the scores are very close. [7]At least, that was the way it had been up until last night. [8]Then the team was playing its most disastrous game of the year.

[9]Last night State plays Podunk University. [10]PU was a small school and almost always has the worst football team in the conference. [11]This season has been no exception. [12]PU's team lost nearly all of its games. [13]Was it any wonder that SU's team thinks it will have an easy time defeating PU?

EXERCISE 12-B

In the paragraphs below, there are a number of errors involving verb forms and the times they indicate (inappropriate switching between past and present, disagreement with the time signal, wrong tense for the time implied, etc.). Find the errors, correct them, and then rewrite the passage. Do not add, remove, or change any words except aux-words and verb forms.

A DISASTROUS GAME—PART II

[1]Last night, however, PU is giving SU a big surprise. [2]If I am not there myself, I don't believe it. [3]In fact, I still can't quite believe what happens. [4]PU beats SU, and the score is 39 to 6!

[5]I suppose SU's team has not been ready for the game—mentally or physically. [6]The coach later has confessed that they are concentrating on their upcoming game with the Bull Run Buffaloes, another championship contender, and give little attention to preparing for the Podunk game. [7]For that reason, during the week before the PU game, some of the SU players have not trained as they should have been. [8]In fact, the night before the PU game, some of them have broken training rules and stayed out late at a wild party.

[9]There has been a lesson to learn from this experience. [10]No matter how good you had been, you could never relax and let your guard down. [11]I will hope SU's players will remember that. [12]Next week they are playing Littleton University, another school with a football team that usually lost. [13]But if SU was not careful it may lose another easy game and, with it, the championship.

EXERCISE 12-C

In the paragraphs below, there are a number of errors involving verb forms and the times they indicate (inappropriate switching between past and present, disagreement with the time signal, wrong tense for the time implied, etc.). Find the errors, correct them, and then rewrite the passage. Do not add, remove, or change any words except aux-words and verb forms.

THE BIRTH OF AN ISLAND

[1]On the morning of November 14, 1963, a small fishing boat cruises off the coast of the Westman Islands in Iceland. [2]Suddenly, the crew felt their boat swayed and they were smelling a strange odor. [3]They were seeing smoke coming from the surface of the ocean a few miles to the south. [4]The captain have thought it might

be a burning ship, so he had his boat heading that way. But the black smoke has come from something else—a volcanic eruption. [6]Before the captain's eyes, as he watches through binoculars, a new island has been born.

[7]Soon, many other people will hurry to see the sight, and modern scientists will have a special opportunity. [8]For the very first time,they will be able to observed a volcanic island's birth and growth.

[9]Several days before the sighting, 425 feet below the surface, an undersea volcano has torn open the rock on the bottom of the ocean. [10]Hot gas, ash, and rock have spewed out. [11]They have formed the base of the new island that will become known as Surtsey. [12]Within a few days, this rapidly growing base will reach the surface of the ocean.

[13]Of course, the eruption was not stopping then. [14]The volcano had continued to spew out ash and lumps of hot lava. [15]By the morning of the second day, the new island grows to a height of 33 feet above sea level. [16]Four days later, it has become even larger—200 feet high and 2,000 feet long. [17]In the next few months, Surtsey had grown until its cliffs had towered hundreds of feet above the Atlantic.

[18]By 1967 the island has been more than a mile long, and its peaks will reach a height of nearly 600 feet. [19]Finally, the lava flows stop. [20]By that time, a new phase in the island's development had begun also. [21]Plants have started to grow in cracks in the rocks, sea creatures are making their homes on Surtsey's beaches, and birds make their nests in the cliffs. [22]Surtsey would begin to mature.[23]Within a few years it will look like other islands around Iceland. [24]But scientists had not forgotten what they will learn from watch Surtsey grow from a column of smoke to a large, rocky island. [25]They enjoy a rare opportunity. [26]They are witnessing a new island's birth.

7

The Sentence

This chapter will help you avoid or correct mistakes like these:

- I met Judy and Richard they are students from Maine.
- Wendy likes Italy, last year she spent three weeks there.
- All the tankers, they need to be tested before being put in service.
- He studies karate, he's a brown belt, it is called lama kai.
- I could not find at the crowded beach my friends.
- He didn't get any mail, but I got ___.
- I need that ball. Please throw ___ me.
- Let's go sit the table.
- That man looks in trouble.
- The meal Joe cooked tasted awfully.
- Let's keep clean the neighborhood!

147

1. Subject and Predicate

In order to write a sentence, you need two things: (1) something to write about; and (2) something to say about it. These are usually called (1) the **subject** and (2) the **predicate.** Each of these can be the length you choose:
from very short (one word each):

Sue / won.

to very long:

> The maximum price for a primary fish shipper sale of fresh fish or seafood (except shrimp, salmon or halibut) to a retailer or purveyor of meals where the sale is negotiated or made at a branch warehouse as herein defined and where the fish or seafood is sold and delivered from the stock of a primary fish shipper wholesaler's branch warehouse which is remote from his main place of doing business, and at which warehouse the primary fish shipper employs two or more full-time employees who are stationed at and engaged in making sales and performing services solely for the primary fish shipper from such warehouse / is the price listed in Table D in 22 plus the allowance provided in 6 for a service and delivery sale where such sale is made, plus the transportation allowance in 9 plus the appropriate container allowance in 21.

(It is not recommended that you write sentences like this "monster," which came from a government manual.)

2. Simple and Complex Sentences

2.1 A simple sentence has one subject and one predicate. Correct simple sentences are fundamental to acceptable writing. They can be combined in a variety of ways to make longer, complex sentences.

> **Simple sentences:**
>   Trees are one of nature's most versatile creations.
>   Trees vary in size.
>   Trees vary in density.
>   Trees grow under many different circumstances.
>   Trees grow at many different rates.
>
> **Combined:** Growing under many different circumstances and at many different rates, trees, one of nature's most versatile creations, vary in age, size, and density.

2.2 A complex sentence can be broken down into simple sentences. (This skill may be useful in increasing reading comprehension.)

> **Combined:**
> Walking to class this morning, George, my friend, stumbled, dropped his books, and lost his math homework, which he had worked on all night.
>
> **Simple sentences:**
> George walked to class this morning.
> George is my friend.
> George stumbled.
> George dropped his books.
> George lost his math homework.
> George worked on his math homework all night.

In this book you will learn to write correct, simple sentences. In Book II (*Sentence Combination*), you will learn a number of ways to combine the simple sentences you have learned to write in this book.

3. Shifters

3.1 **Shifters** are words or groups of words that occur at the beginning or end of a sentence but are not part of the basic sentence. They provide extra information about the basic sentence, such as **time, reason, condition,** or **contrast.** They are called shifters because they can be moved from the front position to the end position, or vice versa, without a change in meaning.

time	Before the race, John exercised daily. John exercised daily before the race.
reason	Because they were afraid of failing, the students didn't even try. The students didn't even try because they were afraid of failing.
condition	If it rains, there will be no ball game. There will be no ball game if it rains.
contrast	Even though he had problems, John kept on trying. John kept on trying even though he had problems.

3.2 To make a yes/no question from a statement that has a front shifter, move the shifter to the end position before moving the aux-word in front of the subject.

> Last summer George couldn't find a job.
> George couldn't find a job last summer.
> Couldn't George find a job last summer?
>
> Because she didn't study, Mary failed the test.
> Mary failed the test because she didn't study.
> Did Mary fail the test because she didn't study?

3.3 Generally front shifters are separated from the basic sentence by commas. However, with many short (less than four words) shifters, no comma is needed. When the shifter appears at the end of a sentence, commas are seldom used. (Shifters and how to create them are discussed in more detail in Chapter 12.)

EXERCISE 3-A   *Make yes/no questions from the following sentences. Be sure to move the shifters from the front to the end of each sentence before moving the aux-words.*

A DECISION

1. For a high school graduate, deciding whether to continue in school or go to work is a momentous decision.

2. Before making a decision, the graduate must consider many things.

3. First of all, finances can be a problem.

4. In making the decision, the availability of jobs becomes a factor.

5. If one decides to go on to college, the selection of a career is important.

6. Next, one should consider the time it may take to earn a degree.

7. After that, one must decide which college or university to attend.

8. If one is going abroad to study, obtaining the necessary passports and visas is an essential step.

9. For many students, military service might be a consideration in making a decision.

10. Everything considered, the decision to continue in school is a difficult one.

EXERCISE 3-B   *Make yes/no questions from the following sentences. Be sure to move the shifters from the front to the end of each sentence before moving the aux-words.*

SPECTATOR SPORTS

1. For many Americans, sports are a reason for living.

2. Every weekend they sit glued to their chairs watching television.

3. In the spring the baseball season starts.

4. In the fall it ends with the World Series.

5. By then the football season is well under way.

6. On Saturdays and Sundays, college and pro games often overlap.

7. All day long one can follow the plays and cheer for favorite teams.

8. On television sports, the best plays can be seen two and three times.

9. After the strenuous games are over, spectators need to walk only a short distance to find food and rest.

10. For anyone who doesn't need exercise, watching sports on television is a great activity.

EXERCISE 3-C   *Make yes/no questions from the following sentences. Be sure to move the shifters from the front to the end of each sentence before moving the aux-words.*

WRITING ENGLISH

1. For many students, writing English is hard.

2. Although they like to talk, they dislike writing.

3. If they would learn the basic skills, writing would not be so hard.

4. First of all the student must recognize that speaking and writing are different arts.

5. As a starter, a student should learn the verb forms and their particular uses.

6. Along with this, a student needs to learn to substitute correct pronouns.

7. After that he should develop the ability to write simple sentences correctly.

8. If he can do that, he should have no trouble learning how to combine sentences.

9. After all the mechanics have been mastered, individual style can be developed.

10. In the end, good sentences make good paragraphs, and well-written paragraphs become good essays.

4. Basic Sentence Patterns

There are four basic sentence patterns in English. All consist of a subject and a predicate. If a **timeless** verb form is used in any pattern it **must** be preceded by an aux-word.

4.1   SENTENCE PATTERN NUMBER ONE

Subject +	(Aux-word) +	Verb$_t$ +	Object
My father John The boss Alfred	is	loves watching insists wants	my mother. (noun) television. (noun) that we work late. (noun clause) to go home. (noun phrase)

4.2   SENTENCE PATTERN NUMBER TWO

Subject +	(Aux-word) +	Verb$_i$
Georgia Mr. Harris	can	giggles. come.

4.3   SENTENCE PATTERN NUMBER THREE

Subject +	(Aux-word) +	Verb$_L$ +	Complement
Marianne He She They	might	seems appear looks seem	tired. (adjective) intelligent. (adjective) like a scholar. (*like* + noun) to be scholarly (*to* + verb)

4.4   SENTENCE PATTERN NUMBER FOUR

Subject +	(Aux-word) +	be +	Complement
My rich uncle He His money	has	is been is	an old man. (noun) very sick. (adjective) in stocks and bonds. (prepositional phrase)

Each of these patterns is discussed in more detail later in this chapter.

EXERCISE 4-A   *Write the number of the sentence pattern used (1, 2, 3, or 4) in each sentence below.*

TESTS—PART I

_____ **1.** I like tests.

_____ **2.** They are a lot of fun.

_____ **3.** I feel happy when I am taking a test.

_____ **4.** This seems strange to most people.

_____ **5.** They think that I am crazy.

_____ **6.** Tests are challenging.

_____ **7.** I study hard before taking a test.

_____ **8.** Sometimes I make mistakes.

_____ **9.** I learn from my mistakes.

_____ **10.** Teachers give tests for many reasons.

_____ **11.** Some like to punish students.

_____ **12.** Others want to measure their students' knowledge.

_____ **13.** My teachers don't know that I like tests.

_____ **14.** I don't tell my secret to them.

_____ **15.** They might not give any more tests to me.

EXERCISE 4-B   _Write the number of the sentence pattern used (1, 2, 3, or 4) in each sentence below._

TESTS—PART II

_____ **1.** I hate tests.

_____ **2.** Teachers give tests all the time.

_____ **3.** Tests bother me.

_____ **4.** I feel sick.

_____ **5.** My head spins.

_____ **6.** I want to run away.

_____ **7.** I still try hard.

_____ **8.** I can't think while taking a test.

_____ **9.** Teachers don't understand.

_____ **10.** They seem indifferent to my feelings.

_____ **11.** They say that I must take tests.

_____ **12.** I feel worse.

_____ **13.** I suffer in silence.

_____ **14.** I try everything.

_____ **15.** I still fail.

_____ **16.** I leave the classroom quietly.

_____ **17.** I feel like an idiot.

_____ **18.** No one understands me.

_____ **19.** Someday they will learn that I am really smart.

_____ **20.** I am not as stupid as they think.

EXERCISE 4-C   _Write the number of the sentence pattern used (1, 2, 3, or 4) in each sentence below._

THE WORLD FOOD PROBLEM

_____ **1.** Everyone must eat.

_____ **2.** Some areas have plenty of food.

_____ **3.** In other places, food is very scarce.

_____ **4.** They don't have enough food to go around.

_____ **5.** Food costs vary from place to place.

_____ **6.** In some countries a person must spend almost all his wages for food for himself and his family.

_____ **7.** Even then they must sometimes go without enough to eat.

_____ **8.** In other places people spend less than ten percent of their income for food.

_____ **9.** Some places grow abundant crops.

_____ **10.** Many people appear overfed.

_____ **11.** They are overweight.

_____ **12.** Some places do not have very much food.

_____ **13.** Sometimes people cannot pay for the available food.

_____ **14.** People frequently die from starvation.

_____ **15.** Many people in the world are concerned about this.

_____ **16.** If we work together, perhaps we can do something about the world food problem.

5. Sentence Pattern Number One

5.1 The most commonly used sentence pattern in English is sentence pattern number one.

Subject	+ (Aux-word) +	Verb	+ Object
We		admired	him.
The president	has	made	a promise.
Our team	will	win	the game.

5.2 Verbs in pattern number one *must* be followed by an object. They are called *transitive* verbs. In most dictionaries the abbreviation *vt* means the verb is transitive (requires an object). The following are some common transitive verbs (they usually take objects):

get (when it means "obtain" or "receive")	do
	make
set	elect
lay	demand
raise	like
have	want
thank	bring
love	threaten

5.3 Do not confuse objects with other words at the end of a sentence. One way to determine if a noun is really an object is to change the sentence into a *wh*-question (see section 11) using *what* or *whom*. In most cases, the word that answers that question is the object. Words that answer *where, why, how,* or *when* questions are not objects; they are used adverbially.

> He saw a movie yesterday.
> **What** did he see yesterday? A movie. (object)
>
> He went home yesterday.
> **What** did he go yesterday? (no answer = no object)
> **Where** did he go yesterday? Home. (adverb)
> **When** did he go home? Yesterday. (adverb)

EXERCISE 5   *Write (in list format) ten simple, related sentences on one of the topics given below. Follow basic sentence pattern number one for all of your sentences. Use time-included forms or aux-words and timeless verb forms. Make sure that each sentence is error-free! Put the headings below at the top of your paper.*

Subject   (Aux-word)   Verb (transitive)   Object

5-A   **games** or **dating**

5-B   **careers** or **politics**

5-C   **cultures** or **marriage**

6. Sentence Pattern Number Two

Subject + (Aux-word) +   Verb

Subject + (Aux-word) + Verb		
Alexander		travels.
Profits	should	increase.

6.1   Verbs in this pattern do *not* take objects. They are called *intransitive* verbs. In most dictionaries the abbreviation *vi* means the verb is intransitive. The following are some common intransitive verbs (they do not usually take objects):

go	sit	laugh
lie	rise	arrive
come	travel	cry
happen	sleep	occur
live	exist	stay

Note: In this book, transitive and intransitive verbs are defined in terms of **function,** not **meaning.**

He *throws* the ball. (Transitive verb. Sentence pattern number one)
      vt

He *throws* well. (Intransitive verb. Sentence pattern number two)
      vi

EXERCISE 6   *Write (in list format) ten simple, related sentences on one of the topics given below. Follow basic sentence pattern number two for all of your sentences. Make sure that each sentence is error-free! Put the headings below at the top of your paper.*

Subject   (Aux-word)   Verb (intransitive)

6-A   **exercise** or **work**

6-B   **travel** or **death**

6-C   **time** or **study**

7. Transitive/Intransitive Verbs

7.1   Some verbs are **transitive** and **intransitive.** In other words, they may or may not take objects. They may be used in either sentence pattern number one or pattern number two.

7.2   Adverbs* and/or prepositional phrases of place, time, and manner (usually in that order) may be added to any basic sentence (many of these adverbs and phrases function as shifters). Any nouns in these phrases are objects of the preposition and **not** objects of the verb.

vt	He	walked	the dog	yesterday.	
		(vt)	(object)	(adverb)	
vi	He	walked	a mile	yesterday.	
		(vi)	(adverb)	(adverb)	
vt	The	policeman	stopped	the car.	
			(vt)	(object)	
vi	The	car	stopped.		
			(vi)		
vt	I	run	the movie projector	at school	every day.
		(vt)	(object)	(adverb)	(adverb)
vi	I	run	five miles	every day.	
		(vi)	(adverb)	(adverb)	

*Adverbs usually answer the questions *when?, how?,* and *where?*

EXERCISE 7-A   *In the passage below, underline each transitive verb (or transitive verb group) and write* vt *above it. Circle the complete object of each transitive verb. Underline each intransitive verb (or intransitive verb group) and write* vi *above it. The first one has already been done for you.*

A BASEBALL GAME

[1]John always <u>enjoys</u> (a good baseball game.) [2]He attends whenever he has a chance. [3]Last night's game thrilled him. [4]The home team was playing against their biggest rival. [5]The fans filled the stands. [6]The home team had been winning. [7]Then a batter hit a line drive. [8]The ball hit the pitcher. [9]It injured his arm. [10]The new pitcher did not have sufficient time to warm up. [11]A home run put the other team in the lead. [12]In the next inning, the pitcher warmed up. [13]He fanned three batters in a row. [14]In the last inning, the home team rallied. [15]A home run with the bases loaded tipped the score in favor of the home team. [16]John went home happy.

EXERCISE 7-B   *In the passage below, underline each transitive verb (or transitive verb group) and write* vt *above it. Circle the complete object of each transitive verb. Underline each intransitive verb (or intransitive verb group) and write* vi *above it. The first one has already been done for you.*

ORIGAMI

¹Have you ever *vt* made (a paper crane?) ²If so, you have encountered the art of origami (Japanese paper folding). ³One must have lots of patience to master this art. ⁴Origami experts must practice for years. ⁵They can easily forget the art.

⁶You may use any kind of paper. ⁷The stiff, shiny, colored squares make the prettiest folded objects. ⁸However, the real beauty of the object depends on the skill of the folder.

⁹Origami relaxes many people. ¹⁰It comes naturally to them. ¹¹It can drive others crazy! ¹²They can't succeed no matter how hard they try.

EXERCISE 7-C   *In the passage below, underline each transitive verb (or transitive verb group) and write* vt *above it. Circle the complete object of each transitive verb. Underline each intransitive verb (or intransitive verb group) and write* vi *above it. The first one has already been done for you.*

THE GREAT BLIZZARD

¹On the morning of Sunday, March 11, 1888, people in New York City were *vi* rushing (home from church meetings.) ²A cold rain was falling on the city. ³No one expected a great blizzard. ⁴The newspaper had predicted clear weather. ⁵Strange things were happening in the atmosphere. ⁶A body of icy cold air more than 1,000 miles long was sweeping down from Canada. ⁷It brought freezing temperatures to the entire eastern third of the United States. ⁸The cold front stretched from New England to Florida. ⁹It met a front of warm, wet air from the south. ¹⁰The heavy rain changed to blinding snow. ¹¹Soon hurricane winds were ripping the Eastern seaboard. ¹²The storm struck Washington, D.C. ¹³It buried the capital with snow. ¹⁴The violent winds smashed ships near the shore onto the rocky coast.

¹⁵On Monday morning, thousands of New York workers left their homes. ¹⁶They were going to work. ¹⁷Most of them did not arrive. ¹⁸Some could not even open their front doors. ¹⁹Snow drifts thirty to forty feet high paralyzed the city. ²⁰They even stopped the trains. ²¹Many people acted like heroes that day. ²²They rescued others from the snow and cold.

²³By Wednesday the storm had ended. ²⁴By the next Sunday most of the snow had melted. ²⁵Life was returning to normal. ²⁶The eastern United States had weathered the greatest blizzard in American history.

EXERCISE 7.1   *Write (in list format) ten simple, related sentences on the topic given. Follow either basic sentence pattern number one or basic sentence pattern number two for each of your sentences. Make sure that each sentence is error-free! Write vt above each transitive verb and circle its object. Write vi above each intransitive verb.*

7.1-A   **sports**

7.1-B   **humor**

7.1-C   **geography**

8. Sentence Pattern Number Three

Subject +	(Aux-word) +	Verb$_L$ +	Complement
Those men		look	happy. (adjective)
The food	should	taste	delicious. (adjective)
The steak		tastes	like cardboard (*like* + noun)
It		appears	to be tender (*to* + verb)

8.1   Verbs used in this pattern are called **linking verbs** because they connect the subject and the complement. The following are some common linking verbs (they take adjective complements).

seem	appear
smell	look
feel	sound
taste	become (may also take a noun complement)
	get (when it means "become")

8.2   Linking verbs are intransitive. When these verbs are used with an object their meaning changes. (They are then used in pattern number one.)

vt   I   smell   the food.   (pattern number one)
            (vt)   (object)

vL   The   food   smells   good.   (pattern number three)
                         (vL)   (adj.)   (The food is not doing the smelling.)

vt   I   feel   the sandpaper.   (pattern number one)
            (vt)   (object)

vL   The   sandpaper   feels   rough.   (pattern number three)
                             (vL)   (adj)   (The sandpaper is not doing the feeling.)

8.3   When *like* follows the linking verb, noun complements may also be used.

This steak tastes like cardboard.

8.4   *to* + verb phrases (traditionally called **infinitives**) may also follow some linking verbs (such as *seem* and *appear*).

> He seems to be tired.

EXERCISE 8   *Write (in list format) ten simple, related sentences on one of the topics given below. Follow basic sentence pattern number three for all of your sentences. Make sure that each sentence is error-free! Put the headings below at the top of your paper.*

Subject   (Aux-word)   Verb (linking)   Adjective

8-A   a place where people eat

8-B   a place where people dance

8-C   a person you know well

9. Sentence Pattern Number Four

Subject	+ Aux-word *be* +	Complement
Dr. Rogers	is	a surgeon. (noun)
The elephants	are	enormous. (adjective)
The students	are	in the library. (prepositional phrase)*

*The locatives *here, there, home, anywhere,* and *everywhere* may be substituted for the prepositional phrase complement.

9.1   In this pattern there are three possible kinds of complements—*nouns, adjectives,* or *prepositional phrases.*

9.2   In addition to the aux-word *be,* other aux-words may also be used. In these cases the form of *be* is determined by the preceding aux-word.

Subject	+ Aux-Word +	*be* +	Complement
That man	may (time-included)	be (timeless)	the thief. (noun)
That dog	might (time-included)	be (timeless)	sick. (adj.)
Jack	could (time-included)	be (timeless)	in the bookstore. (prep.phrase)
My grandfather	has (time-included)	been (timeless)	a doctor for many years. (noun + adverb)
George	has (time-included)	been (timeless)	sick. (adj.)
They	have (time-included)	been (timeless)	at home. (prep. phrase)
Jeannette	is (time-included)	being (timeless)	funny. (adj.)

Note: A noun complement is not the same as an object. In fact, it is essentially the same thing as the subject. (Subject pronouns are used in complement position.)

Objects and subjects are **not** related by the action of the verb.

EXERCISE 9   *Write (in list format) twelve simple, related sentences on one of the topics given below. Follow basic* sentence pattern number four *for all of your sentences. Use* noun complements *in four sentences,* adjective complements *in four sentences, and* prepositional phrase complements *in four sentences. Label each sentence,* N, A, *or* P *depending on the kind of complement you use. Make sure that each sentence is error-free.*

9-A   a famous person

9-B   a famous place

9-C   a famous thing

10. Variations on Basic Sentence Patterns

10.1   The four sentence patterns presented in this chapter are the basic sentence patterns in English. All other sentences are *variations,* *transformations,* or *combinations* of these basic patterns.

10.2   One common variation is the **addition** of a noun, adjective, or verb **complement to an object** (in a pattern number one sentence). This complement describes or shows the action of the object, not the subject, of the sentence.

Subject +	Vt +	Object +	Complement
Barbara	called	Stephen	a coward. (noun complement)
The PTA	appointed	John	chairman. (noun complement)
The students	made	Sally	embarrassed. (adjective complement)
They	painted	their house	yellow. (adjective complement)
That movie	made	me	cry. (verb complement)
We	heard	the dogs	bark(ing). (verb complement)

When the object complement is a verb, only timeless base and *-ing* verb forms are used (*d-t-n* verb forms may be used as adjectives). Time-included verb forms are never used as complements to objects.

> Sad stories make Terry *cry*. (**not** *cries*)
> We saw the cat *climbing* (**not** *climbed*) the tree.

10.3   The **passive** and **indirect object transformations** are discussed in Chapter 10. Here are a couple of examples:

> John was hit by a car. (Passive formed from pattern no. 1: A car hit John.)
> John gave Mary a present. (Indirect object transformation from pattern no. 1: John gave a present to Mary.)

10.4 Various types of **combinations** are discussed in Book II. Here are examples of three common sentence combinations.

> Snow White married Prince Charming, and they lived happily ever after. (From sentence pattern no. 1, "Snow White married Prince Charming," and sentence pattern no. 2, "They lived happily ever after.")
>
> Although the weather was fine, they stayed home. (From sentence pattern no. 4, "The weather was fine," and sentence pattern no. 2, "They stayed home.")
>
> Jumping up from his seat, George shook his fist at the man. (From sentence pattern no. 2, "George jumped up," and sentence pattern no. 1, "George shook his fist at the man.")

10.5 **Inversions** are rarely used in speech but are often found in formal writing. When inversions are used, sentence units do not follow their normal order.

> Never realized was Dorothy's ambition to become a movie star. (inverted)
> Dorothy's ambition to become a movie star was never realized. (normal)
>
> Strange though my story may seem, it is true. (inverted)
> Though my story may seem strange, it is true. (normal)
>
> Eligible to apply for the awards are graduating high school seniors. (inverted)
> Graduating high school seniors are eligible to apply for the awards. (normal)

The rules for these inversions are very complex and depend on a number of factors such as vocabulary, emphasis, original sentence construction, register, and style. It is not recommended that you use them in your writing at this stage. However, you should be able to recognize inversions when you see them in writing.

EXERCISE 10 *Using* only *the four basic sentence patterns (and the complement variation if you wish),* but *no transformations or combinations, write fifteen error-free, related sentences (in list format) about one of the topics given below. Use each of the four basic sentence patterns at least once. Label your sentences (1), (2), (3), or (4) according to the basic sentence pattern you choose to use.*

10-A   your home or room

10-B   a town or city

10-C   your best friend or worst enemy

11. *Wh-* Questions

11.1 *Wh-* questions are sometimes called **information** questions because they require more than a simple *yes* or *no* answer. They are called *wh-* questions because they begin with the question words *who, whom, what, which, where, when, why, whose,* or *how.* Only one of these *wh-* words can be used at a time when forming a question from a basic sentence (which contains the answer to the question).

There are two main *wh-* question patterns:

1. Questions about the **subject** of the sentence, and
2. Questions about **objects or other parts of the predicate** of the sentence.

11.2   SUBJECT QUESTION PATTERN

If the subject of the basic sentence is **human,** simply substitute *who* for the complete subject whether it is singular or plural. When a plural subject is replaced by *who* or *what,* it is common to change the aux-word or verb to its singular form (+*s* form) unless the rest of the sentence indicates that the replaced subject is plural.

John gave my books to Mary. (basic sentence)
Who gave my books to Mary? (*wh-* question) (answer = John)

The boys at the bus stop were waiting impatiently. (basic sentence)
Who was waiting impatiently? (*wh-* question) (answer = The boys at the
bus stop)

If the subject is **non-human,** simply substitute *what* for the complete subject whether it is singular or plural (and, if the replaced subject is plural, change the aux-word or verb to its singular form).

The morning newspaper carried a notice of the meeting on the last page.
What carried a notice of the meeting on the last page?

The *trees in the park* shaded the picnic area.
What shaded the picnic area?

11.3   PREDICATE QUESTION PATTERN

In this pattern the **aux-word** must be moved in front of the subject as it is for yes/no questions. (This is explained in Chapter 4.) The *wh-* word replaces the complete object or other part of the predicate, but it is placed before the aux-word. If the object is **human,** the *wh-* word is *whom.* (*Whom* is rarely used in speech, but it is common in formal writing.) If the object is **non-human,** the *wh-* word is *what.*

Dr. Anderson addressed *the students* in the assembly.
Whom did Dr. Anderson *address* in the assembly?
(*wh-*) (hidden aux-word) (base form)

The morning newspaper carried *a notice of the meeting on the last page.*
What did the morning newspaper *carry* on the last page?
(*wh-*) (hidden aux-word) (base form)

Other *wh-* question words are used as substitutes for other parts of the predicate:

---

where for place
when for time
why for purpose or reason
how for manner (also *how much* and *how many* for quantity)
whose for possessives (the accompanying noun is also moved to the front of
the sentence)

As with the *whom* or *what* replacement, these *wh-* words are placed at the beginning of the sentence followed by the aux-word.

> John gave my books to Mary *in front of the library.* (place)
> *Where* did John give my books to Mary?
>
> John gave my books to Mary *after school.* (time)
> *When* did John give my books to Mary?
>
> John *quickly* gave my books to Mary. (manner)
> *How* did John give my books to Mary?
>
> John gave my books to Mary *because he had to catch the bus.* (reason)
> *Why* did John give my books to Mary?
>
> John gave *my* books to Mary. (possessive)
> *Whose* books did John give to Mary?

When the word being replaced by the *wh-* word is the **object of a preposition,** *whom* (for humans) or *what* (for non-humans) is used. In formal usage, the preposition is also moved to the front and precedes the *wh-* word.

> John gave my books *to Mary.* (preposition and object of preposition)
> *To whom* did John give my books?

The word *which* is used when **choosing from a group** of people or things. It is often followed by the word *of* and a plural noun. (Although the noun is plural, the aux-word or verb agrees with the singular *which.*)

> Here are some new styles. *Which* do you prefer?
> *Which* of these books is yours?

How is often followed by other adjectives to ask special information questions (e.g., *how far* for distance, *how hot* for temperature, *how old* for age, etc.).
What occasionally replaces adjectives in forming questions (e.g., *what color, what building*).

EXERCISE 11-A   *Make up an exam about the following passage by substituting* wh- *words for the underlined parts of each sentence. (The underlined parts will be the answers to the questions you create.) You may use pronouns in your questions. Write your seventeen questions on a separate sheet of paper.*

A RADIO DRAMA

Many people were listening to a radio program one evening in 1938.
$\overline{}$ $\quad$ $\overline{}$ $\quad$ $\overline{}$
   1   2   3

This program was broadcast before television sets were common household
$\overline{}$ $\overline{}$
   4   5

furniture. People heard reports that men from outer space had landed in the
$\overline{}$ $\overline{}$
   6   7

state of New Jersey. The program announced when it started, and again when
$\overline{}$ $\overline{}$
   8   9

it <u>ended</u>, <u>that the men-from-space landing was completely fictitious.</u>
10

<u>Panic-stricken people</u> crowded narrow highways and tunnels <u>in New Jersey</u>
11   12

<u>that evening.</u> They were trying to escape <u>the fictional invasion.</u> <u>Orson Welles</u>
13   14   15

was <u>the producer of this extraordinary program.</u> Even today, he is remembered
16

for <u>this action-packed radio drama.</u>
17

EXERCISE 11-B   *Make up an exam about the following passage by substituting* wh- *words for the underlined parts of each sentence. (The underlined parts will be the answers to the questions you create.) You may use pronouns in your questions. Write your seventeen questions on a separate sheet of paper.*

FLEET FEET

<u>Many fast running animals</u> live <u>in the wilderness areas of the world.</u>
1   2

<u>Gazelles, cheetahs, and antelope</u> all attain <u>high speeds</u> <u>while running.</u>
3   4   5

<u>The fastest running animal of them all</u> is <u>the fleet-footed cheetah.</u>
6   7

<u>A cheetah</u> can run <u>seventy-one miles per hour</u> <u>as it flees from an enemy.</u>
8   9   10

<u>The fast running cheetah</u> can attain a forty-five-mile-an-hour speed within
11

<u>two seconds</u> from a standing start <u>on the plains.</u> <u>The best cars</u> can't match
12   13   14

<u>that fast start</u> <u>on racing days</u> <u>at the racetrack.</u>
15   16   17

EXERCISE 11-C   *Make up an exam about the following passage by substituting* wh- *words for the underlined parts of each sentence. (The underlined parts will be the answers to the questions you create.) You may use pronouns in your questions. Write your seventeen questions on a separate sheet of paper.*

KING TUT'S TOMB

<u>In 1922,</u> <u>an English archaeologist named Howard Carter</u> was working
1   2

<u>near Cairo, Egypt.</u> He looked through <u>a small hole that he had drilled in the</u>
3   4

<u>wall of a tomb.</u> At first, he saw <u>nothing.</u> Then, as his eyes grew accus-
5

tomed to the light, he began to distinguish <u>the details of the room.</u> He saw
6

<u>strange animals, statues, and gold</u>—everywhere the glint of gold! He had dis-
7

covered <u>the tomb of Tutankhamen, one of the great Pharaohs of ancient Egypt.</u>
8

A clay tablet in the tomb carried the inscription "Death will slay with his wings
         9   10

whoever disturbs the peace of the Pharaoh."

Since 1922, many scientists, archaeologists, and scholars who have worked
                                   11

with King Tut's relics have suffered misfortunes. Over thirty of these people
                               12   13

have died unexpectedly. Many people claim that "King Tut's curse" is
          14   15   16

responsible for every one of these misfortunes. Others do not take the "curse"
                                   17

quite so seriously.

A

Forms of Content Words

This list is by no means complete. For additional words and word forms, consult a good dictionary. Parentheses indicate words rarely, if ever, used. Prepositions in parentheses after verbs indicate normal usage.

Noun	Verb	Adjective	Adverb
ability	enable	able	ably
absence	absent	absent	absently
achievement	achieve	achievable	—
acquisition	acquire	acquisitive	acquisitively
act, activity, action	act	active	actively
adequacy	—	adequate	adequately
admission	admit	admissible	admissibly
advantage	—	advantageous	advantageously
adventure	adventure	adventurous	adventurously
advice	advise	advisory	(advisorily)
aggression	aggress	aggressive	aggressively
aggressor			
allowance	allow	allowable	(allowably)
ambition	—	ambitious	ambitiously
America, American, Americana, Americanism	Americanize	American	—
anger	anger	angry	angrily
appreciation	appreciate	appreciative	appreciatively
appropriation	appropriate	appropriate	appropriately
approximation	approximate	approximate	approximately
arrogance	—	arrogant	arrogantly
art, artistry, artist, artisan	—	artistic	artistically
attention	attend (to)	attentive	attentively
attraction	attract	attractive	attractively
authority	authorize	authoritative	authoritatively
basis	base	basic	basically
beauty	beautify	beautiful, (beauteous)	beautifully
benefit	benefit	beneficial	beneficially
bravery	brave	brave	bravely
breadth	broaden	broad	broadly
brevity, brief	abbreviate	brief	briefly
brilliance	—	brilliant	brilliantly
building, builder	build	—	—
capability	—	capable	capably
capture, captor	capture	captive	(captively)

Noun	Verb	Adjective	Adverb
center	centralize	central	centrally
challenge, challenger	challenge	challengeable	—
circle	circle	circular	circularly
clarity	clarify	clear	clearly
cleverness	—	clever	cleverly
cloud, cloudiness	cloud up	cloudy	cloudily
comfort	comfort	comfortable	comfortably
communication, communicator, communicativeness	communicate	communicable, communicative	(communicably) communicatively
competition	compete	competitive	competitively
complaint, complainer	complain	—	—
completion, completer, completeness	complete	complete	completely
complex, complexity	—	complex	complexly
comprehension	comprehend	comprehensive	comprehensively
computer	compute	computable	—
compulsion	compel	compulsive	compulsively
confidence	confide (in)	confident	confidently
consideration	consider	considerable	considerably
construction	construct	constructive	constructively
consumption	consume	consumable	—
conversion	convert	convertible	(convertibly)
correction	correct	correct	correctly
correctness corrector	correct	correct	correctly
corruption	corrupt	corrupt	(corruptly)
courage	encourage	courageous	courageously
criminal, criminality	—	criminal	criminally
culture	—	cultural	culturally
curiosity	—	curious	curiously
danger	endanger	dangerous	dangerously
dedication, dedicator	dedicate	dedicatory	—
deduction	deduct	deductible	—
defense	defend	defensive	defensively
definition	define	definitive	(definitively)
delinquency	—	delinquent	(delinquently)
dependence, dependent	depend (on)	dependent	dependently
description	describe	descriptive	descriptively
desire	desire	desirable	desirably
destruction	destroy	destructive	destructively
determination	determine	determinable	—
difference	differ (from)	different	differently
disadvantage	—	disadvantageous	(disadvantageously)
disaster	—	disastrous	disastrously
discovery, discoverer	discover	discoverable	—
disgrace	disgrace	disgraceful	disgracefully
displeasure	displease	—	—
distance	distance	distant	distantly
division	divide	divisible	(divisibly)
domination	dominate	dominant	dominantly
donation, donor, donator, donative	donate	—	—
doubt	doubt	doubtful	doubtfully, doubtlessly
eagerness	—	eager	eagerly
earliness	—	early	early
education	educate	educational	educationally
effect	effect	effective	effectively
emotion	emote	emotional	emotionally
employee, employer, employment	employ	employable	—
endurance	endure	endurable	(endurably)
energy	energize	energetic	energetically
enforcement	enforce	enforceable	enforceably
enthusiasm	enthuse	enthusiastic	enthusiastically
equality	equalize	equal	equally
erection	erect	erect	(erectly)
essence, essentiality	—	essential	essentially
example	exemplify	exemplary	(exemplarily)
excellence	excel	excellent	excellently
exhaustion	exhaust	exhaustive	exhaustively
expanse	expand	expansive	expansively
exploitation	exploit	exploitable	(exploitably)
extension	extend	extensive	extensively

Noun	Verb	Adjective	Adverb
failure, failing	fail	—	—
fame	—	famous	famously
familiarity	familiarize	familiar	familiarly
fatality	—	fatal	fatally
favor	favor	favorite	—
fertility, fertilizer	fertilize	fertile	fertilely
firmness	firm	firm	firmly
flower, floweriness, (flowerage)	flower	flowery, floral, flowerless	(flowerily)
flight, flyer/flier	fly	—	—
force	force	forceful	forcefully
foreigner	—	foreign	(foreignly)
frankness	—	frank	frankly
freedom	free	free	freely
friend, friendliness	befriend	friendly	friendly
gallantry	—	gallant	gallantly
government	govern	governmental	(governmentally)
gradualness	—	gradual	gradually
grievance	grieve	grievous	grievously
happiness	—	happy	happily
harshness	harshen	harsh	harshly
haste	hasten	hasty	hastily
heart	hearten, dishearten	hearty, heartfelt	heartily
height	heighten	high	highly
hero, heroism	—	heroic	heroically
history, historian, (historicalness)	—	historic, historical	historically
honesty	—	honesty	honestly
ignorance	ignore	ignorant	ignorantly
imagination	imagine	imaginative	imaginatively
immediacy	—	immediate	immediately
immensity	—	immense	immensely
importance, import	—	important	importantly
impossibility	—	impossible	impossibly
impression	impress	impressive	impressively
independence	—	independent	independently
indication	indicate	indicative	(indicatively)
individual, individualism, individuality	individualize	individual (istic)	individually
inevitability	—	inevitable	inevitably
influence	influence	influential	influentially
insecurity	—	insecure	insecurely
inspiration	inspire	inspirational	inspirationally
instruction, instructor	instruct	instructional, instructive	instructively
integrity	—	integral	integrally
intelligence	—	intelligent	intelligently
irritation, irritator, irritability, irritant	irritate	irritable, irritative	irritably
Japan, Japanese	—	Japanese	—
jealousy, jealousness	—	jealousy	jealously
joy, joyfulness, joyousness	enjoy	joyful, joyless, joyous	joyfully, joylessly, joyously
justice	—	just	justly
justification, justifier	justify	justifiable	justifiably
keeper, keepsake	keep	keeperless	—
kindness	—	kind, kindly	kindly
knot	knot	knotty	
knowledge, knower	know	knowledgeable	knowledgeably
largeness	enlarge	large	largely
lateness	—	late	lately
laziness	(laze)	lazy	lazily
legality	legalize	legal	legally
legislation, legislator, legislature	legislate	legislative	(legislatively)
length	lengthen	long, lengthy, lengthwise	lengthily
liberty	liberalize	liberal	liberally
liberty, liberation	liberate	—	—
liberality, liberalization	liberalize	liberal	liberally
limitation	limit	limitable	limitably
location	locate	local	locally

Noun	Verb	Adjective	Adverb
looseness	loosen	loose	loosely
loss	lose	lost	—
loyalty	—	loyal	loyally
magnet	magnetize	magnetic	(magnetically)
management, manager	manage	manageable, managerial	manageably
might	—	mighty	mightily
migration, migrant	migrate	migratory	—
minimum	minimize	minimal	minimally
movement	move	movable	—
negation	negate	negative	negatively
newness	—	new, newish	newly
noise, noisemaker, noiselessness	noise	noisy, noiseless	noisily, noiselessly
notice	notice	noticeable	noticeably
obligation	obligate	obligatory	(obligatorily)
observation, observer	observe	observant	observantly
occasion	occasion	occasional	occasionally
occupation	occupy	occupational	(occupationally)
offense, offender	offend	offensive	offensively
opportunity, opportunist	—	opportune	opportunely
opposition, opposite	oppose	opposite	(oppositely)
oppression, oppressor	oppress	oppressive	oppressively
optimism, optimist	—	optimistic	optimistically
paint, painter, painting	paint	—	—
part	part	partial	partially
peace, pacifism, pacifier	pacify, pacificate	peaceful, pacific, peaceable	peacefully, peaceably
permission, permit	permit	permissive	permissively
perpetuation	perpetuate	perpetual	perpetually
person, personality	personalize	personal	personally
persuasion	persuade	persuasive	persuasively
politics (always pl.), politician	—	political, politic	politically
possession, possessor	possess	possessive	possessively
poverty	impoverish	poor	poorly
prediction	predict	predictable	predictably
preparation	prepare	preparatory	—
prevention	prevent	preventive	(preventively)
product, produce, producer, production, productivity	produce	productive, producible	productively
profit	profit	profitable	profitably
prohibition	prohibit	prohibitive	prohibitively
provision	provide	provisional	provisionally
quickness	quicken	quick	quickly
recurrence	recur	recurrent	recurrently
reduction, reducer, (reducibility)	reduce	reducible	(reducibly)
regularity	regularize	regular	regularly
regulation	regulate	regulative	(regulatively)
relation, relative	relate	relative	relatively
reliance, reliability	rely (on)	reliable	reliably
remedy	remedy	remedial	(remedially)
reminiscence	reminisce	reminiscent	(reminiscently)
research, researcher	research	researchable	—
respect	respect	respectful, respective	respectfully, respectively
response, respondent	respond	responsive	responsively
responsibility	—	responsible	responsibly
resistance	resist	resistant	(resistantly)
revelation, revealer, revelator	reveal	revelatory, revealable	(revealably)
rivalry, rival	rival	rival	—
satisfaction	satisfy	satisfactory	satisfactorily
scorn	scorn	scornful	scornfully
secrecy	—	secretive	secretively
section	sectionalize, section	sectional	(sectionally)
sentiment, sentimentality	—	sentimental	sentimentally
separation	separate	separate	separately
severity, severeness	—	severe	severely
sharpness	sharpen	sharp	sharply
significance	signify	significant	significantly
silence, silencer	silence	silent	silently
skill		skillful	skillfully

Noun	Verb	Adjective	Adverb
smoothness, smoother	smooth, (smoothen)	smooth	smoothly
solemnity	solemnize	solemn	solemnly
song, singer	sing	songful, songless	songfully, songlessly
steadiness	steady	steady	steadily
strangeness	—	strange	strangely
student	study	studious	studiously
subsidiary, subsidy	subsidize	subsidiary	—
success	succeed	successful	successfully
suddenness	—	sudden	suddenly
suitability	suit	suitable	suitably
suspicion, suspect	suspect	suspicious	suspiciously
swiftness	—	swift	swiftly
symbol	symbolize	symbolic	symbolically
sympathy	sympathize	sympathetic	sympathetically
system	systematize	systematic	systematically
tardiness	retard	tardy	tardily
tax, taxability, taxer	tax	taxable, taxless	(taxably)
technique	—	technical	technically
temporariness	temporize	temporary	temporarily
tightness	tighten	tight	tightly
toleration	tolerate	tolerable	tolerably
tranquility, tranquilizer, tranquilization	tranquilize	tranquil	tranquilly
transference, transfer	transfer	transferable	—
treachery	—	treacherous	treacherously
triumph	triumph (over)	triumphant	triumphantly
tropic(s)	—	tropical, tropic	tropically
trouble, troubler, troublemaker	trouble	—	—
tyranny, tyrant	tyrannize	tyrannical	(tyrannically)
uncertainty	—	uncertain	uncertainly
upset, upsetter	upset	upset	—
victory, victor	—	victorious	victoriously
vigor	invigorate	vigorous	vigorously
virtue	—	virtuous	virtuously
vitality	vitalize	vital	vitally
violence	—	violent	violently
warning, warner	warn	—	—
watchman, watch, watcher, watchfulness	watch	watchful	watchfully
whiner, whine	whine	whiny	whiningly
work, worker, workability	work	workable	(workably)
writing, writer, (writ)	write	—	—
yawn, yawner	yawn	—	yawningly
year, yearling	—	yearly, yearlong	yearly
yellow	yellow	yellow	—
youngster	—	young, youngish	—
zeal, zealot, zealotry	—	zealous	zealously
zest	(zest)	zestful, zestless	zestfully, zestlessly

B

Some Common Noncount Nouns and Unit Expressions

advice (piece)
anger (fit, pique)
beauty
bacon (slice, pound)
baggage (piece, set)
beef (piece, slice, side, pound, kilo, serving, platter, helping, can, tin)
beer* (bottle, glass, mug, can, vat, keg)
bread (slice, loaf)
biology**
butter (pat, cube, tub, pound)
cardboard (piece, sheet)
catsup (bottle, dab, teaspoon, cup)
cereal (box, package, bag)
chalk (piece, box)
cheese (piece, slice, head, pound)
chemistry**
cloth* (yard, bolt, meter, piece, scrap, sample)
clothing (piece)
cocoa (cup, mug, glass, teaspoon, can, serving)
concrete (yard, bag, wheelbarrow)
cream (cup, pint, half-pint, bottle, carton, teaspoon, tablespoon)
corn* (ear, field, bushel, can, kernel)
coverage
difficulty*
detergent (box, cup, squirt, cup)
economics**

emphasis
exercise* (hour, minutes, session)
entertainment (night, hour)
fabric* (yard, meter, bolt, piece, scrap, sample)
film* (roll, box, package, can, reel)
flour (sack, bag, pound, cup)
fluid (drop, teaspoon, tablespoon, ounce, cup, quart, gallon, bottle, can, barrel)
fog* (day, week)
foil* (roll, sheet)
food* (plate, serving, mouthful, can)
furniture (piece, room, set)
garlic (clove, tooth)
gas (gallon, cubic foot)
geometry**
glass* (piece, pane, sheet)
gold (ounce, bar, bag)
grass (field, clump, blade)
gravy (bowl, boat, ladle, pan, serving)
gossip* (piece)
hair* (strand, head, handful, shock)
ham* (serving, slice, helping, ounce, pound, kilo, platter)
homework (page, ton)
hamburger* (pound, patty)
honey (jar, spoonful, can, comb, pound)
ice cream (half-gallon, carton, tub)
ink (bottle, cartridge)
intelligence (grain, ounce, lick [colloquial])

iron* (ton, pound, truckload, piece)
jam (jar, spoonful, ounce)
jealousy (fit, pique, attack)
jewelry (piece, set)
juice (glass, pitcher, cup, quart, gallon)
junk (piece, pile, truckload)
lamb* (leg, slice, piece, pound, kilo, shoulder)
leather (piece, strip, square inch)
lemonade* (glass, pitcher, cup, quart, gallon)
lettuce (head, leaf)
lipstick (tube)
love*
luggage (piece, set)
luck (piece)
lumber (piece, board foot, truckload)
mail (piece, bag, shipment)
makeup
material (*see* fabric)
mathematics**
meat (pound, kilo, serving, slice, platter, bite, helping)
medicine* (dose, teaspoon, drop) [also**]
milk* (glass, quart, gallon, bottle, carton)
money
news (piece)
oil (drop, teaspoon, ounce, cup, quart, can, barrel)
oxygen (breath, tank)
paper (sheet, piece, package, ream)
pepper (pinch, dash, spoon)
photography**
perfume* (ounce, bottle)
polish* (can, bottle, ounce)
pork (serving, slice, roast, loin, side, helping, pound, kilo, platter)
powder (box, can, keg)
pride (ounce)
power*
pressure*

rain* (inch, drop, day, week)
ribbon* (inch, foot, yard, piece, roll)
rice (grain, cup, pound, bag, sack)
rope (foot, yard, length, coil)
salt (teaspoon, tablespoon, spoonful, pinch, dash, ounce)
sand (grain, bucket, yard, shovelful)
sight*/***
silver (ounce, bar, bag)
skin*
sleet
smell*/***
snow* (inch, foot, ton)
soap (bar, box, drop, squirt)
soup (bowl, tureen, ladle, spoonful, can, tin, pot)
stuff (box, pile, room, load, yardful)
sugar (sack, bag, pound, cup, spoon)
tape* (roll, piece, inch, foot, yard)
time* (minute, second, hour, day, week, month, year, century, millennium, eon)
tin* (sheet, piece, square inch)
toast* (piece, slice)
toothpaste (tube, tin, squeeze)
touch*/***
tuition
tread (fraction of an inch)
vision*/***
vocabulary*
water* (drop, ounce, glass, cup, quart, gallon, bucket, cubic foot, acre foot)
weight* (gram, ounce, pound, kilo, ton)
wax (can, bottle)
wheat (grain, ear, bag, pound, ton)
wind* (gust)
wine* (bottle, carafe, glass, drop)
wood (piece, stick, load, cord)
work (minute, hour, day, piece, lick [colloquial])

*These nouns are normally noncount, but they can also be count nouns. When they are count nouns, the meaning is different from the noncount meaning (see Chapter 2, sections 1.5 and 1.6).
**These are areas of study. Unit expressions are not normally used with them. However, unit expressions relating to courses, books, etc. (e.g., area, branch, course, unit, page) are sometimes used with them.
***Senses do not normally use unit expressions.

APPENDIX

C

Irregular Verb Forms

TIMELESS			TIME-INCLUDED		
				Present	Past
Base	**d-t-n**	**-ing**	**+s**	**No-s**	
be	been	being	is	am, are	was, were
bear	borne, born	bearing	bears	bear	born
beat	beaten, beat	beating	beats	beat	beat
become	become	becoming	becomes	become	became
begin	begun	beginning	begins	begin	began
bend	bent	bending	bends	bend	bent
bet	bet	betting	bets	bet	bet
bite	bitten, bit	biting	bites	bite	bit
bleed	bled	bleeding	bleeds	bleed	bled
blow	blown	blowing	blows	blow	blew
break	broken	breaking	breaks	break	broke
bring	brought	bringing	brings	bring	brought
build	built	building	builds	build	built
burst	burst	bursting	bursts	burst	burst
buy	bought	buying	buys	buy	bought
catch	caught	catching	catches	catch	caught
choose	chosen	choosing	chooses	choose	chose
come	come	coming	comes	come	came
cost	cost	costing	costs	cost	cost
creep	crept	creeping	creeps	creep	crept
cut	cut	cutting	cuts	cut	cut
deal	dealt	dealing	deals	deal	dealt
dig	dug	digging	digs	dig	dug
dive	dived	diving	dives	dive	dived, dove
do	done	doing	does	do	did
draw	drawn	drawing	draws	draw	drew
drink	drunk	drinking	drinks	drink	drank
drive	driven	driving	drives	drive	drove

TIMELESS			TIME-INCLUDED		
			Present		**Past**
Base	*d-t-n*	*-ing*	**+ s**	**No-s**	
eat	eaten	eating	eats	eat	ate
fall	fallen	falling	falls	fall	fell
feel	felt	feeling	feels	feel	felt
fight	fought	fighting	fights	fight	fought
find	found	finding	finds	find	found
flee	fled	fleeing	flees	flee	fled
fly	flown	flying	flies	fly	flew
forget	forgotten	forgetting	forgets	forget	forgot
forgive	forgiven	forgiving	forgives	forgive	forgave
freeze	frozen	freezing	freezes	freeze	froze
get	got, gotten	getting	gets	get	got
give	given	giving	gives	give	gave
go	gone	going	goes	go	went
grow	grown	growing	grows	grow	grew
hang	hung	hanging	hangs	hang	hung
hang (a person)	hung	hanging	hangs	hang	hanged
have	had	having	has	have	had
hear	heard	hearing	hears	hear	heard
hide	hidden	hiding	hides	hide	hid
hit	hit	hitting	hits	hit	hit
hold	held	holding	holds	hold	held
hurt	hurt	hurting	hurts	hurt	hurt
keep	kept	keeping	keeps	keep	kept
kneel	knelt, kneeled	kneeling	kneels	kneel	knelt, kneeled
know	known	knowing	knows	know	knew
lay	laid	laying	lays	lay	laid
lead	led	leading	leads	lead	led
leave	left	leaving	leaves	leave	left
lend	lent	lending	lends	lend	lent
let	let	letting	lets	let	let
lie (recline)	lain	lying	lies	lie	lay
lie (tell an untruth)	lied	lying	lies	lie	lied
light	lighted, lit	lighting	lights	light	lighted, lit
lose	lost	losing	loses	lose	lost
make	made	making	makes	make	made
mean	meant	meaning	means	mean	meant
meet	met	meeting	meets	meet	met
pay	paid	paying	pays	pay	paid
put	put	putting	puts	put	put
quit	quit	quitting	quits	quit	quit
read	read	reading	reads	read	read
ride	ridden	riding	rides	ride	rode
ring	rung	ringing	rings	ring	rang
rise	risen	rising	rises	rise	rose
run	run	running	runs	run	ran
say	said	saying	says	say	said
see	seen	seeing	sees	see	saw
seek	sought	seeking	seeks	seek	sought
sell	sold	selling	sells	sell	sold
send	sent	sending	sends	send	sent
set	set	setting	sets	set	set
shake	shaken	shaking	shakes	shake	shook
shine (shoes)	shined	shining	shines	shine	shined
shine (sun)	shone	shining	shines	shine	shone
shoot	shot	shooting	shoots	shoot	shot

TIMELESS			**TIME-INCLUDED**		
			Present		**Past**
Base	*d-t-n*	*-ing*	**+ s**	**No-s**	
shrink	shrunk	shrinking	shrinks	shrink	shrank
shut	shut	shutting	shuts	shut	shut
sing	sung	singing	sings	sing	sang
sink	sunk	sinking	sinks	sink	sank
sit	sat	sitting	sits	sit	sat
slay	slain	slaying	slays	slay	slew
sleep	slept	sleeping	sleeps	sleep	slept
wake	waked, woken	waking	wakes	wake	waked, woke
wear	worn	wearing	wears	wear	wore
weave	woven	weaving	weaves	weave	wove
weep	wept	weeping	weeps	weep	wept
win	won	winning	wins	win	won
wind	wound	winding	winds	wind	wound
wring	wrung	wringing	wrings	wring	wrung
write	written	writing	writes	write	wrote

APPENDIX

D

Some Common Phrasal Verbs

Inseparable

call on—ask to recite
catch up (with)—reach, come even with, return to schedule
come back—return
come over—visit
come up with—invent, create mentally
drop out (of)—stop attending
fall behind—lag, fail to stay together with or on schedule
fool around—play aimlessly
get along (with)—cooperate, relate harmoniously
get along—progress
get around to—find time to, finally start to
get away (with)—escape detection
get by—succeed with little effort
get into—become involved in
get out (of)—escape, evade
get over—recover
get through (with)—finish
get up—arise
go on—happen
go over—review
keep on—continue
keep up with—stay even with, stay on schedule
look for—seek
look into—investigate
look out—beware
make out—succeed, survive
make sure (of)—verify
make up—reconcile

Separable

back up—move to the rear
blow open—open with explosives
blow up—destroy with explosives
break up—separate (two people)
call on—visit, ask to participate
call up—call on the telephone
chop down—chop an object until it falls
chop up—chop completely (into pieces)
clean up—clean thoroughly
do over—repeat
fill out—complete (a form)
fill up—fill completely (to capacity)
give back—return (something to someone)
give up—surrender, cease
gobble down—eat quickly and completely
hand in—submit (something to someone)
hand out—distribute (something to a group)
hang up—terminate telephone connection
help out—help (informal)
hold up—rob
hook up—connect
hurry up—make happen faster
keep up—maintain
leave behind—abandon
leave on—allow to remain operating
leave out—omit
let go—release
look over—examine
look up—search for

Inseparable

make up for—compensate
pull up (at a place)—arrive
run across—discover by chance
run into—meet by chance
run out (of)—exhaust the supply
run over—hit with a vehicle
show up—appear
sit down—sit completely
stand up—stand completely
take part (in)—participate
think of—invent, create mentally
turn over—rotate
wait for—wait (for something/somebody)

Separable

make (one's mind) up—decide
make up—prepare, invent
mix up—confuse
open up—open completely, begin
pick out—choose
pick up—lift, raise, gather
pin down—locate, identify
put (clothing) on—dress
put away—return to proper place
put off—postpone
put out—extinguish
put up—raise
run down—lose power
run up—accumulate
show off—display
start up—cause to begin operating
take apart—disassemble
take down—record in writing
take off—remove, undress
take out—remove from an area
take up—introduce, discuss
talk over—discuss
try out—test thoroughly
turn off—cause to stop operating
turn on—cause to start operating
use up—use completely (until none remains)
wake up—awaken

APPENDIX

E

Exercise Titles

CHAPTER ONE

2-A	Ancient American Ruins
2-B	Flowering Trees
2-C	Foreign Language Study
3-A	Early Americans
3-B	Art
3-C	Taxes
3.1-A	Culture Shock
3.1-B	Computers
3.1-C	Cultural Adjustment
4-A	Flying in a Sailplane
4-B	Handling Angry Feelings
4-C	How to Get Fired

CHAPTER TWO

1-A	Party Preparations
1-B	Losing Weight
1-C	Homework Blues
1.1-A	This Class
1.1-B	Your Car
1.1-C	The News
1.2-A	Summer Camp
1.2-B	Classmates
1.2-C	Hobbies
2-A	What Did You Buy?—Part I
2-B	What Did You Buy?—Part II
2-C	What Did You Buy?—Part III
4-A	Lunchtime
4-B	Friends
4-C	Gaining Knowledge
5-A	A Traffic Incident
5-B	The Lion and the Mouse
5-C	The Lion and the Donkey

5.1-A	A Stagecoach Ride—Part I
5.1-B	A Stagecoach Ride—Part II
5.1-C	A Stagecoach Ride—Part III
7-A	A Short Vacation
7-B	A Quick Trip Around the World—Part I
7-C	A Quick Trip Around the World—Part II
8-A	Cultural Differences and International Trade—Part I
8-B	Cultural Differences and International Trade—Part II
8-C	Cultural Differences and International Trade—Part III

CHAPTER THREE

1-A	Davy Crockett—Part I
1-B	Davy Crockett—Part II
1-C	Davy Crockett—Part III
2-A	Tokyo
2-B	Mount Fuji
2-C	Hokkaido
3-A	Oceans
3-B	Typewriters
3-C	Constantine
4-A	A Cold Day
4-B	A Garden
4-C	Daydreams
4.1-A	Fairy Tales
4.1-B	The Circus
4.1-C	The Iceman
4.2-A	Tonight's Newspaper
4.2-B	The Circus
4.2-C	Personal Management